Hotel Crescent Court, A Rosewood Hotel
& The Spa at the Crescent
(See related stories pages 53 & 63.)

Salon at Eaton Court
(See related story page 213.)

The Corinthian
Bed & Breakfast
(See related story page 36.)

Photos by Dan Tucker

Photo by Nick Inglish

Barron's Fine Jewelry
(See related story page 155.)

Nature's Finest Art
(See related story page 205.)

The Atrium at the Granville Arts Center
(See related story page 234.)

The Old Craft Store

Mary Lou's Gifts and Collectibles

Ten of Arts

Softwear Embroidery

The Finishing Touch Mall

CARROLLTON TEXAS

COMMUNITY MERCHANTS

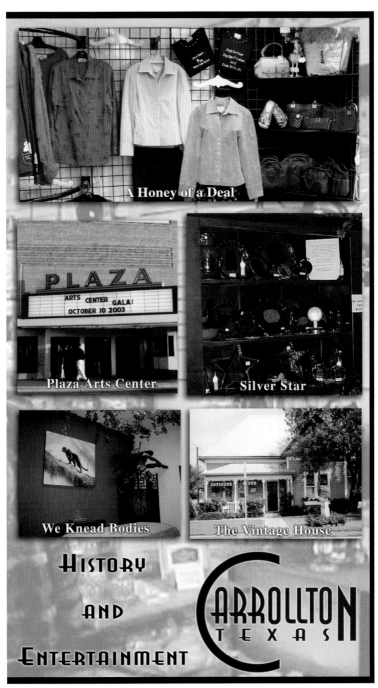

A Honey of a Deal

PLAZA
ARTS CENTER GALA!
OCTOBER 10 2003

Plaza Arts Center

Silver Star

We Knead Bodies

The Vintage House

HISTORY

AND

ENTERTAINMENT

CARROLLTON
TEXAS

(See related story page 67.)

City of McKinney
(See related story page 178.)

Sweet Tomato
(See related story page 191.)

THE WOOLIE EWE
(See related story page 212.)

Photo by Phillip Ray Sharp

City of Lewisville
(See related story page 161.)

Babe's Chicken Dinner House & Bubba's Cooks Country
(See related stories pages 59, 78, & 232.)

City of Rockwall
*(See related story
page 215.)*

Photo by Zane Toombs

Miss Olivia's
(See related story page 147.)

Photo by Karen Estes

Courtesy of Cooke County Heritage Society

City of Gainesville
(See related story page 137.)

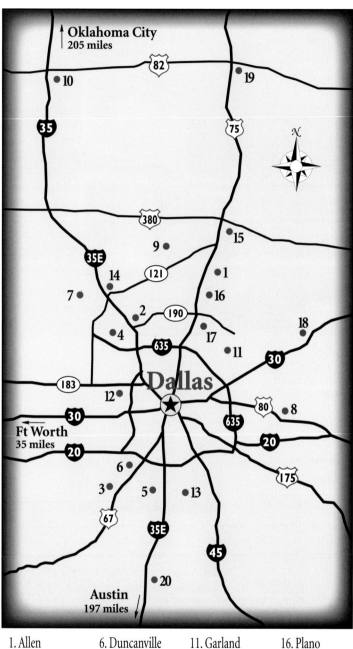

1. Allen
2. Carrollton
3. Cedar Hill
4. Coppell
5. DeSoto
6. Duncanville
7. Flower Mound
8. Forney
9. Frisco
10. Gainesville
11. Garland
12. Irving
13. Lancaster
14. Lewisville
15. McKinney
16. Plano
17. Richardson
18. Rockwall
19. Sherman
20. Waxahachie

Available Titles

After enjoying this book, we are sure you will also love our other books:

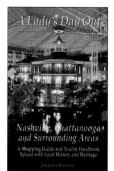

"A LADY'S DAY OUT IN NASHVILLE, CHATTANOOGA AND SURROUNDING AREAS"

From the rolling hills and mountains to Music City USA or the world's largest freshwater aquarium, Tennessee has got it going on! Discover Tennessee like you've never experienced it, with the help of our 19th book. "A Lady's Day Out in Nashville, Chattanooga and Surrounding Areas." You'll find the best shopping, lodging, eating and pampering services that each town has to offer, while learning the area's history, its special attractions, its extraordinary people and its calendar of events. This book is a must-have for those planning a getaway to: Nashville, Chattanooga, Bell Buckle, Brentwood, Clarksville, Clifton, Cookeville, Crossville, Dickson, Fayetteville, Franklin, Gallatin, Goodlettsville, Hendersonville, Lawrenceburg, Lebanon, Leipers Fork, Lynchburg, Murfreesboro, Pickwick, Savannah, Shelbyville, Signal Mountain and Waynesboro. — *280 pages - $19.95*

"A LADY'S DAY OUT ON NORTHWEST FLORIDA'S EMERALD COAST"

Sparkling, emerald green waters along miles of pristine sugar white sand beaches make the Emerald Coast breathtaking! You'll find beachside restaurants, shopping treasures, relaxing accommodations and sun-kissed attractions among the unhurried world along the Gulf. This book is the perfect companion guide to adventurers exploring the warmth and hospitality of Apalachicola, Carillon Beach, Destin, Fort Walton Beach, Grayton Beach, Gulf Breeze, Mexico Beach, Navarre Beach, Niceville, Pace, Panama City Beach, Pensacola, Pensacola Beach, Port St. Joe, Rosemary Beach, Sandestin, Santa Rosa Beach, Seagrove Beach, Seaside, Shalimar and Valparaiso. — *237 Pages - $19.95*

"A LADY'S DAY OUT IN THE RIO GRAND VALLEY AND SOUTH PADRE ISLAND"

Discover why the Rio Grand Valley and South Padre Island are the perfect places for a "two-nation vacation"! With one set of roots planted deeply in Mexico, and the other firmly in Texas, this book is loaded with magnetic "Beinvenidos" appeal. Tourists from the Northern United States flood to the Valley during the winter months to enjoy the warmer temperatures and delightful lifestyle. Vibrant shopping, casual eateries, charming attractions and wonderful accommodations makes this book a must have when planning an afternoon, weekend or week long get-away in Alamo City, Brownsville, Edinburg, Harlingen, Hidalgo, La Feria, Los Fresnos, McAllen, Mission, Pharr, Port Isabel, Port Mansfield, Raymondville, Reynosa, Rio Grande City, Roma, South Padre Island, and Weslaco. — *176 Pages - $19.95*

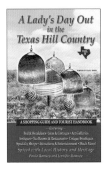

"A LADY'S DAY OUT IN THE TEXAS HILL COUNTRY, VOLUME II"

Spiced with local history and heritage; this book is our latest edition for the Texas Hill Country. Featuring the best bed & breakfasts, inns, cottages, art galleries, antiques, tea rooms, restaurants, unique boutiques, specialty shops, attractions and entertainment the Hill Country has to offer. Find out why the Texas Hill Country is a favorite destination for all. Plan your trip by using this book and you'll be sure to guide yourself to the best and most unique towns and shops the Hill Country has to offer. Featuring the wonderful towns of Bandera, Boerne, Medina, Vanderpool, Blanco, Brady, Brownwood, Early, Burnet, Buchanan Dam, Comfort, Fredericksburg, Goldwaite, Hamilton, Johnson City, Stonewall, Junction, Kerrville, Ingram, Lampasas, Llano, Marble Falls, Kingsland, Mason and Wimberley. — *250 Pages - $18.95*

"A LADY'S DAY OUT IN MISSISSIPPI"

Southern charm and uniqueness drip from the pages of this Shopping Guide and Tourist Handbook. We have found true Mississippi treasures! As always great shopping, dining and lodging fill the pages of this book in this fascinating state. Bay St. Louis, Biloxi, Canton, Cleveland, Columbus, Jackson, Natchez, Ocean Springs, Oxford, Pass Christian, Picayune, Vicksburg and Waveland are all covered. — *212 Pages - $17.95*

"A LADY'S DAY OUT IN TEXAS, VOL. III"

Features 37 new "GET-A-WAY" Texas towns—most are new and not covered in Texas, Vol. II—brimming with fascinating history and delightful, unique shopping. Inside you'll find all the details about romantic bed & breakfasts and inns, fabulous antique shops, lovely art galleries, home décor, gift shops and exciting entertainment, tea rooms, soda fountains and much more. — *276 Pages - $18.95*

"A LADY'S DAY OUT IN TEXAS, VOL. II"

Let us guide you through the highways and by-ways of Texas through 27 HISTORIC TOWNS & CITIES. True to form we have found the best shopping, dining, bed & breakfasts and inns in great, not so well known "GET-A-WAYS." — *346 Pages - $17.95*

— BOOKS SOON TO BE AVAILABLE —
"A Lady's Day Out in Atlanta, Georgia & Surrounding Areas"
"A Lady's Day Out in Northern New Mexico"

Book Order Form

A Lady's Day Out, Inc.
8563 Boat Club Road
Fort Worth, Tx 76179
Toll Free: 1-888-860-ALDO (2536)

Please send _____ copies of **"A LADY'S DAY OUT IN DALLAS & SURROUNDING AREAS, VOL. II"** at $19.95 per copy, plus $2.00 postage for each book ordered. (Tax included.)

Please send _____ copies of **"A LADY'S DAY OUT IN NASHVILLE, CHATTANOOGA & SURROUNDING AREAS"** at $19.95 per copy, plus $2.00 postage for each book ordered. (Tax included.)

Please send _____ copies of **"A LADY'S DAY OUT ON NORTHWEST FLORIDA'S EMERALD COAST"** at $19.95 per copy, plus $2.00 postage for each book ordered. (Tax included.)

Please send _____ copies of **"A LADY'S DAY OUT IN THE RIO GRANDE VALLEY & SOUTH PADRE ISLAND"** at $17.95 per copy, plus $2.00 postage for each book ordered. (Tax included.)

Please send _____ copies of **"A LADY'S DAY OUT IN THE TEXAS HILL COUNTRY, VOL. II"** at $18.95 per copy, plus $2.00 postage for each book ordered. (Tax included.)

Please send _____ copies of **"A LADY'S DAY OUT IN MISSISSIPPI"** at $17.95 per copy, plus $2.00 postage for each book ordered. (Tax included.)

Please send _____ copies of **"A LADY'S DAY OUT IN TEXAS VOL. III"** at $18.95 per copy, plus $2.00 postage for each book ordered. (Tax included.)

Please send _____ copies of **"A LADY'S DAY OUT IN TEXAS VOL. II"** at $17.95 per copy, plus $2.00 postage for each book ordered. (Tax included.)

Please send _____ copies of **"A KID'S DAY OUT IN THE DALLAS/FORT WORTH METROPLEX, VOL. I"** at $16.95 per copy, plus $2.00 postage for each book ordered. (Tax included.)

MAIL BOOKS TO:

NAME: _____

ADDRESS: _____

CITY_____ STATE_____ ZIP_____

AMOUNT ENCLOSED: _____

CREDIT CARD ORDERS CALL: 1-888-860-ALDO (2536)

A Lady's Day Out

in

Dallas & Surrounding Areas

VOLUME II

A Shopping Guide & Tourist Handbook

— featuring —

Allen • Carrollton • Cedar Hill • Coppell • Dallas
DeSoto • Duncanville • Flower Mound • Forney
Frisco • Gainesville • Garland • Irving • Lancaster
Lewisville • McKinney • Plano • Richardson
Rockwall • Sherman • Waxahachie

by Jennifer Ramsey

Cover features Hotel Crescent Court, A Rosewood Hotel
(See related story on page 53.)

CREDITS

Editor/Author
Jennifer Ramsey

Director of Research & Sales
Jennifer Ramsey

Editor & Writer
Michelle Medlock Adams

Contributing Writers
Jenny Harper Nahoum
Gena Maselli
Jill Boyce

Administrative & Production
Kay Payne
Mary Manzano
Laura Pender

Research & Sales
Jennifer Stierwalt
Kendall Corder
Sharon Campbell
Tere Carter
Tina Lynch

Copyright 2005
A Lady's Day Out, Inc.
ISBN: 1-891527-16-9

Paid advertising by invitation only.

Produced by
A Lady's Day Out, Inc.

Printed in the United States of America
By Armstrong Printing Company, Austin, Texas

Table of Contents

Note from the Author

I'm always excited when we have a new release of the "A Lady's Day Out" series, but I am especially thrilled to offer you this book because it's about my home state of Texas. Recently, Florida and Tennessee have demanded a large portion of my time. Although these states have much to offer, as I am sure you know if you have read "A Lady's Day Out on Northwest Florida's Emerald Coast" or "A Lady's Day Out in Nashville, Chattanooga and Surrounding Areas"—it is always good to be home.

Dallas—The Big "D"—has long been known in Texas and throughout the country as "The Place" to find sophistication, style and overall panache. Sometimes, this type of notarity comes with accompanying negative adjectives such as: snobbish, impersonal and cold. But, I want to squash those misconceptions like a bunch of grapes in the winepress. Dallas needs to be known for its heart and soul. Yes—Dallas drips with sophistication, style and panache, but Dallas and its surrounding areas should also be recognized for their warmth and compassion. Dallas should be known for the heart and soul of the amazing people who call this place home. From the city limits of Dallas to the charming surrounding towns, we have found the best of the best. Some locations we've chosen to highlight are already well known, but others are not so well known…yet. In the following pages, you will not only discover wonderful places, but also wonderful people. You'll meet the people who not only live here, but also have exciting, clever and must-see businesses. I know you will enjoy this book—whether you are a visitor to Dallas or a Texas native. Of course, if you're a visitor, here's a word of caution. Many visitors quickly become natives, because the Texas charm holds them hostage. Well, that's OK. We welcome you.

Enjoy your shopping, dining, and overall "fun" while in Dallas. You deserve it! Trust me; I have highlighted the best for you in this book. I challenge you, though, to look beyond what you can put into a sack and carry home with a pretty red bow (we all know that will be wonderful). Look deeper into the heart and soul of these kind and incredibly talented business owners—people who are fulfilling their dreams and enabling you to enjoy some of your own. Investigate and meditate. We did, and we liked what we saw. This is what Dallas is truly all about. Enjoy!!!

Jennifer "Jenni" Ramsey

Dallas and Surrounding Areas

Think big! Then think bigger! "Big" is the operative word here, and the first word that comes to mind for this incredible Lone Star city. "Big D," "Bigger 'n Dallas," "Big Tex." The adjective not only describes the size of the city (which, of course, is very big), but encapsulates the way of life that is Dallas. Everything about Dallas exceeds expectation or imagination. From the glitz that makes it one of the nation's most glamorous fashion meccas, to the blue-and-silver studded football helmets of "America's Team"—Dallas is bigger than life.

Dallas Through the Decades

Dallas is an intriguing mix of modern sophistication, cultural diversity and true Southern hospitality, so it is no wonder that it is one of the top visitor destination cities in all of Texas. In fact, the "larger than life" state of mind that permeates every part of present-day Dallas was the impetus behind its very beginnings. In 1841, Mr. John Neely Bryan established a trading post on the bank of the Trinity River. He had migrated to this area from Tennessee, and loved the rolling prairie and native pecan and cottonwood trees along the river. He claimed 640 acres and sketched out a town that would grow to be larger than anything he could have ever imagined. In fact, more than one million people now live in Dallas, and more than two million in Dallas County. Sadly, the origin of the name "Dallas" has never been verified. Archives reveal only that it was named for "John Neely Bryan's friend." This could have been George Mifflin Dallas, Vice President under President James K. Polk; Commodore

Alexander James Dallas, a naval commodore stationed in the Gulf of Mexico; Walter R. Dallas, who fought at San Jacinto and had land holdings near Bryan; James L. Dallas, a Texas Ranger; or Joseph Dallas, a friend from Bryan's hometown. Mr. Bryan never managed to verify Dallas' namesake before his death in 1877. Be sure to visit John Neely Bryan's restored log cabin located in downtown Dallas.

Outlaws

When the Houston & Texas Central Railroad chugged into town in 1872, with the Texas & Pacific Railway right behind in 1873, they brought with them a population explosion that has never stopped. New businesses and buildings sprang up overnight, and telegraph lines connected Dallas with the world. Of course, along with the fast population growth and increasing popularity came problems common to the West during this time—outlaws. Belle Star began her career as a dance hall singer in Dallas, but later harbored outlaws and made a living selling stolen horses. The famous gunfighter and gambler Doc Holliday hung his dentistry shingle in Dallas during the 1870s, but practiced at cards more than dentistry. These were the days of cattle drives and dusty rodeos, of gunfights and gamblers, and miles and miles of open range. Dallas was the personification of "West" to the world, and still is today. It has just blended that Old West charm with modern sophistication and Southwestern warmth.

Neiman Marcus

Just a few decades after the railroads changed the history of Dallas, Neiman Marcus was founded in the downtown area in 1907 by Mr. Herbert Marcus, his sister Carrie Marcus Neiman, and her husband Al Neiman. Herbert's son Stanley Marcus joined the family business during the 1920s, shepherding in an excitement about retail that completely changed the future of Neiman Marcus and Dallas. In fact, shortly after the opening of the remarkable Neiman Marcus store, Mr. J.S. Armstrong opened his exclusive Highland Park shopping development in the northern part of the city. The Marcus family's high standards for quality, and the desire for unsurpassed customer service, still govern the way they do business today. Mr. Marcus created the Neiman Marcus Award for Distinguished Service in the Field of Fashion in 1938, which has been presented through the years to top designers such as Coco Chanel, and individuals who have drastically influenced fashion. Baby boomers will remember the beginning of the legendary "His" and "Hers" gifts in 1960, and the excitement of receiving the internationally renowned Neiman Marcus Christmas Book each year.

Oil Boom!

The 1930s ushered in, or should we say, "gushered in" the oil boom in Texas. Marion "Dad" Joiner struck oil just 100 miles east of Dallas, which was the beginning of the famous East Texas Oil Field, the largest petroleum deposit on earth at that time. Although Dallas County has never had a working oil well itself, it has had the role of being the financial and technical center for a lot of the state's drilling industry. After Dad Joiner's oil discovery, new businesses moved to Dallas; banks were established for loans to develop the oil fields; and Dallas became the financial center for oil fields in East Texas, the Permian Basin, the Gulf Coast, the Panhandle and Oklahoma. The "Thirties" was also the decade that saw the completion of developments like Fair Park, which won the bid to host the Texas Centennial Exposition in 1936. Today, this beautiful complex is home to nine exciting museums, and it hosts the largest exposition in all of North America.

A Changing Skyline

Perhaps the years that had the largest impact on the economy of Dallas were the 1960s. It was during this time that Dallas and Fort Worth agreed upon a joint effort to build an airport that would serve the entire region. It was the completion of the gigantic DFW International Airport that made Dallas a major inland port. At that time in history, the skyline of downtown Dallas began its transformation. Football's Dallas Cowboys began their ascent to fame during the 1960s, and Coach Tom Landry became one of the most admired men in America. Entrepreneur Mary Kay Ash began selling beauty products in the suburban homes of Dallas during the 60s, turning a small home party selling program into a billion dollar makeup company. Even today, several years after her death, the name Mary Kay and the company's signature "pink Cadillacs" are recognizable throughout the world. This would also be the decade that saw incredible growth of the Dallas Market Center, and the opening of Six Flags Over Texas in nearby Arlington.

The Loss of a Hero

Unfortunately, history would also unconsciously blame Dallas for the loss of its hero, President John F. Kennedy. November 22, 1963, is a day that many Americans can point to as a defining time in their lives. They remember exactly where they were and what they were doing when the news was broadcast over radio and television that President Kennedy had been assassinated in downtown Dallas. The tragic death of one of the most revered presidential figures in history cast a terrible light on the city, and Dallas fought hard through a period of deep evaluation and introspection. It has succeeded in preserving the inspirational legacy President Kennedy left behind, and the site of his death has since been turned into a place of historical commemoration of this crucial event in history. In 1969, a close friend of the Kennedy family, Mr. Phillip Johnson, constructed the John F. Kennedy Memorial on Main and Elm streets downtown. It is a 50 square foot open-roofed, concrete monument, which was designed by former First Lady, Jacquelyn Kennedy Onassis. The Sixth Floor Museum at Dealey Plaza in downtown Dallas—the location from which Lee Harvey Oswald allegedly shot the president—features historic photographs, artifacts and documentary film on the life, death and legacy of John F. Kennedy.

Destination Dallas and Surrounding Areas

At the conclusion of the 1980s, *Fortune Magazine* named the Dallas/Fort Worth area the No. 1 business center in the land. The city had garnered international attention as the leading convention destination in the United States and as a leader in the tourism industry. On a lighter note, this was also the decade that prompted people from around the world to ask the question, "Who Shot J.R.?" The South Fork Ranch, where visitors can tour the famous Ewing mansion from the hit T.V. drama "Dallas," is still a favorite attraction on any visitor's itinerary.

The recent renovation and rejuvenation of downtown Dallas has kept it a major center for entertainment and art, and, of course, unsurpassed shopping opportunities. Dallas now boasts the largest wholesale market in the world, and it's the Southwest's leading business and financial center. The 21st Century continues to see phenomenal growth and expansion of the Dallas/Fort Worth area, as it holds its honor as being one of the top visitor destinations in Texas.

Dallas is certainly the core of the North Central Texas Region, but exceptional opportunities for recreation and family entertainment lie within the neighboring communities that are blended into one "big" exciting experience. Surrounding lakes and reservoirs provide excellent fishing and boating, and sporting enthusiasts may experience one of six professional sporting events through the year. Dallas has been rated in the top 10 for sports in the United States by *The Sporting News* since 1992. There are professional football, baseball, basketball, and indoor and outdoor hockey teams, as well as several universities that provide exciting, competitive sporting opportunities.

Of course, Dallas conjures up images of the first trail riders and cowboys that shaped its early days, so visitors still expect to see remnants of the real West when they visit. There are also many wonderful western "Dude Ranches" throughout the area that allow weekends of Wild West fun for the entire family.

The areas that surround Dallas provide a variety of entertainment opportunities as varied as the colors in the Texas sky. Head to Gainesville to visit the famous Frank Buck Zoo, or drive to Plano to see the sky filled with hundreds of Hot Air Balloons. Just a few miles away, antique lovers can browse for days on end in Forney, "The Antique Capital of Texas."

Dazzling Dallas is a deeply woven fabric of beauty and culture, glitz and glamour, legend and lore. You can be shopping the most sophisticated clothing and jewelry boutiques by day, and doing the Texas Two-Step in an authentic honky-tonk that same night. You will see that, indeed, everything really is "bigger" in Texas, and that "Big D" offers more shopping, recreation, adventure and fun than any other place in Texas. You will be thrilled with all of the wonderful and exciting adventures available in Dallas and the surrounding areas. You will find treasures and trifles you "just can't live without." You will learn history and get a glimpse into the future of this dynamic city. You might spend your time enjoying the different zoos and theme parks nearby. Or, you might even saddle up for a trail ride at a dude ranch. No matter what you do, you'll be impressed with the people who call Dallas "home." Whether they are the mom and pop owners of a soda fountain shop in a tiny nearby town, a fancy tearoom owner in one of the city's upscale neighborhoods, or a docent on a downtown tour, they all have one thing in common—they are Texans. And, they all have "big" hearts that welcome all to their beautiful Lone Star state.

Dallas / Take One!

The warm climate, wide-open ranges, and towering skyscrapers have attracted moviemakers to Dallas for decades. Here is a list of just some of the movies and TV series you might recognize that were filmed right here in Dallas.

1945 – *State Fair*
1967 – *Bonnie & Clyde*
1974 – *Benji*
1976 – *Logan's Run*
1978-1991 – *Dallas TV Series*
1983 – *Tender Mercies and Silkwood*
1984 – *Places in the Heart*
1987 – *Robocop*
1988 – *It Takes Two*
1988 – *Talk Radio*
1989 – *Born on the 4th of July*
1992 – *Ruby*
1993-2001 – *Walker, Texas Ranger*
1997 – *The Apostle*
1997 – *Batman & Robin*
1999 – *Any Given Sunday*
          Boys Don't Cry
          Universal Soldier
2000 – *Dr. T. and the Women*
2002 – *The Rookie*
2003 – *Saving Jessica Lynch*
2004 – *The Benefactor*

Diamonds of Dallas – Its People

CAROLINE ROSE HUNT

She is a mother, grandmother, great grandmother, author, accomplished gourmet cook, and one of the most respected businesswomen in Texas and throughout the United States. Her achievements and accolades are almost too numerous to list, and she has been the recipient of coveted awards from organizations and non-profit companies throughout the nation. Caroline Rose Hunt is the woman behind Rosewood Hotels & Resorts, which manages 14 properties, including The Mansion on Turtle Creek, Hotel Crescent Court in Dallas and the Carlyle in New York City. She is also co-founder of Lady Primrose's Royal Bathing & Skin Luxuries and Lady Primrose's Shopping English Countryside.

Entering the world in 1923, Ms. Hunt was born into the Texas version of royalty. Her father was Texas oil billionaire H.L Hunt. She received her Bachelor of Arts degree from the University of Texas at Austin, and holds Honorary PhDs from Mary Baldwin College and the University of Charleston. Caroline Rose Hunt has authored several books, including "The Compleat Pumkin Eater," 1980, "Primrose Past," 2001, and "A Family Cooks," 2002. She has also been a contributing author to *Aura Magazine*, and *High Society Magazine*.

Known as "the Grande Dame of Dallas Society," Caroline Rose Hunt has given so much to Dallas over the years—her time, her talents and her good fortune. She was the founder and chairman of the Legacy Circle of United Way of Dallas in 1999, and she currently sits on the boards of the National Museum of Women in the Arts, Mary Baldwin College, the Junior League of Dallas and the Crystal Charity Ball. She remains active in Highland Park Presbyterian Church, the Dallas Symphony Orchestra Scroll Society, the Junior League, the Dallas Women's Club, the Dallas Historic Society, Daughters of the American Revolution, the Dallas Arboretum Society, and the Dallas Heritage Society.

Throughout her career, Caroline Hunt has received prestigious honors including Distinguished Women's Award, Northwood Institute–1983, Award for Excellence in Community Service in the Field of Business, Dallas Historical Society–1984, American Food and Wine Institute Award–1988, Les Femmes du Monde Award–1988, National Fragrance Council Award–1994, British American Commerce Association Award–1996, Trolley Hall of Fame Award–1998, Texas Trailblazer Award by the Family Place–2003, Arts Patronage Award, Museum of Women in the Arts–2003, and the Lifetime Community Achievement Award by the Los Angeles Junior League–2004. She was named one of six "Texas Tycoons and Tastemakers" by *Ultra Magazine,* and "Style Setter" by *Texas Homes Magazine.* In addition, she was inducted into the Texas Business Hall of Fame.

As you can see by this incredible and only partial list of Ms. Hunt's accomplishments, she is quite the go-getter. Her tireless energy and enthusiasm for life, and her care and concern for people, have fueled her determination to make the world a better place. Along the way, she has also managed to make the world a more beautiful place. In fact, her Rosewood Hotels have been named some of the top hotels in the world, with the latest being the magnificent Hotel Crescent Court here in Dallas. It has been described as "18th century French classical architecture—a lacy, limestone and cast-aluminum hotel, shopping center and office tower which boasts glassware from Germany, silver-plated wine buckets from Brazil, copper pots from Portugal, bed linens from Belgium, and 10 types of marble from Italy and Spain." Ms. Hunt then teamed with friend and business partner Vivian Wilcox Young to create the beautiful "Lady Primrose's Shopping English Countryside," a magnificent store in fantasy setting, featuring decorative accessories and gift items, antique furniture and the Lady Primrose's Royal Bathing & Skin Luxuries.

Lovers of history and all things Victorian will enjoy Caroline Hunt's extraordinary book, "Primrose Past," which recreates Victorian England through the diary of a young girl in 1848. The text of the journal includes a present-day narrative in Caroline's own voice, which details the discovery of the actual diary and her attempts to discover the truth behind the story. The book was published by HarperCollins/Regan Books in 2001.

Caroline Rose Hunt has accomplished more than most people can even dream about during their lives. She has touched the hearts and lives of so many with her generosity and kindness, and she has inspired the business community with her forward thinking vision for Dallas. It is no surprise that *Ladies Home Journal* named her "One of America's 100 Most Influential Women" in 1983. She is truly one of the Lone Star state's most distinguished treasures.

H. ROSS PEROT

When *Dallas Morning News* recently asked H. Ross Perot what attributes he hoped people would give at his funeral, he answered, "I would like my funeral to be a celebration, not a mourning event, focused on: I had the finest parents anyone could have; I have the world's best wife; I have five wonderful children; I have 15 perfect grandchildren; and, I had great people in my companies who carried me on their shoulders from one victory to another, and made my companies successful." H. Ross Perot is a self-made billionaire philanthropist who sold his company, Data Systems, Corp., to General Motors in 1984 for $2.5 billion. He ranks 73rd on the *Forbes* 400 Richest People in America list, with a net worth today of more than $3.8 billion. He has been called a maverick, tenacious, opinionated and stubborn. His own son, Ross Perot Jr., says of his famous father, "If he thinks he is right, that's all that matters!" It is this "do or die, get-it-done spirit" that has enabled H. Ross Perot to become one of the country's most influential businessmen.

Ross Perot was born in 1930 in Texarkana, Texas, and attended school and junior college there. He entered the United States Naval Academy in 1949 and graduated in 1953. Ross met his wife, Margot

Birmingham, while he was a midshipman at the Naval Academy. After marrying in 1956, they settled in Dallas, where Ross worked for IBM's data processing department, and she taught school. In fact, it was Margot who loaned Ross money from her savings account to start his one-man data processing company, which he named Electronic Data Systems. Today, EDS is a multi-billion dollar corporation. The Perots have remained in Dallas. It was here they raised their five children: Ross, Jr., Nancy, Suzanne, Carolyn and Katherine. Now, Ross and Margot enjoy their 15 grandchildren.

As Ross Perot, Jr., stated, his father's absolute conviction that he is right about what he believes has worked to his benefit all of his life. His moral strength and courage to take action have enabled him to make his dreams come true. And, he has been extremely generous with his good fortune. He received the Medal for Distinguished Public Service in 1972 for his work in helping free POWs in Southeast Asia. He also funded an operation in 1979 to rescue two of his employees from an Iranian prison. He personally went to Iran and walked into the prison where they were being held. He has also funded programs to help make Texas the *least* desirable state for illegal drug operations, and the state with a first-class education system.

H. Ross Perot continued to draw national attention, when in 1992, he emerged as an independent candidate for president of the United States, and finished third in the general election with nearly one-fifth of the popular vote. In 1995, he founded a new national party called the Reform Party, and as the party's 1996 presidential candidate, he again finished third in the election.

Mr. Perot has continued through the years to gain notoriety for his staunch beliefs and convictions, and his one-liners have become quite well known. Here are a few of our favorites:

"If someone blessed as I am is not willing to clean out the barn, who will?"

"If you can't stand a little sacrifice and you can't stand a trip across the desert with limited water, we're never going to straighten this country out."

"If you see a snake, just kill it – don't appoint a committee on snakes!"

"Talk is cheap, words are plentiful. Deeds are precious."

These statements give just a little insight into the personality and strength of Mr. H. Ross Perot, whose deeds have indeed been precious. His work continues to benefit the State of Texas and the United States as a whole, and his "bigger 'n Dallas," never-quit spirit will live on through his family's philanthropic investments. In fact, the Perots have given more than $200 million to charitable and civil causes. He is extremely proud of his 1984 purchase of a copy of the "Magna Carta," which was the only copy allowed out of Great Britain. The document is on loan from the Perot family to the National Archives in Washington, D.C., for display alongside the "U.S. Constitution" and the "Bill of Rights." Businessman, politician, philanthropist, grandpa—you gotta love H. Ross Perot!

PATTY GRANVILLE

Although she wasn't born and bred in Texas, Patty Granville got here as fast as she could, and her talents and contributions to Texas have almost outshined the Lone Star itself! Visitors to Garland, Texas, are greeted almost immediately by what Patty proudly calls, "The Gateway to Garland," and "The Heart of the Community." The incredible Granville Arts Center opened in 1982 as The Garland Center for the Performing Arts, and marked the flourishing of the arts in Garland. Under the direction of Patty Granville, the center surpassed all expectations, winning numerous state awards. Patty's borrowed challenge, "If you build it, they will come," proved true the minute the doors opened in 1982. Today, more than 150,000 people visit the center each year to attend plays, seminars, receptions, musicals and concerts.

Because of Patty's hard work and total commitment to the center, the Garland City Council voted unanimously in 2003 to rename the center, the Patty Granville Arts Center. Council member Jackie Fegin said, "She has been the guiding force. Cities have consulted with her. She is a teacher and a performer." We couldn't agree more, which is why we're recognizing Patty—one of Garland's "1st Ladies"—and a person who has enhanced the arts community of Texas and indeed the entire country.

Patty Granville grew up in West Virginia and found her way to Texas in 1973 and to Garland in 1978. She has extensive background in theatre and TV, founded upon a degree in Theatre and Speech from the College of William and Mary in Williamsburg, Va., and a Masters in Theatre from the University of North Texas. Many will remember her as "Miss Patty" on the syndicated television show "Romper Room" from 1968-1970. Or, you might remember her for her work in area dinner theater and summer musicals. She also worked for KXTX 39 Television for many years, and has been producing the Garland Summer Musicals for more than 22 years.

Patty has been passionate about her work with the Arts Center over the years, where she has served continuously as the executive director of cultural facilities. Ironically, she almost missed out on this great opportunity. In fact, she had just decided to take the LSAT and start law school in 1982 when she was approached about this exciting opportunity. She never pursued the law degree, and she has never looked back. She and her husband Dr. Hamp Holcomb enjoy a blended family of three daughters and five adorable (and very talented, we're sure) grandchildren. She works tirelessly with the Arts Center, yet still finds the time and energy to be involved in the production of the Garland Summer Musicals. She says that her husband even gets involved in a play once in a while, because he shares her enthusiasm for the theatre and for life.

When we asked Patty, "How does it feel to have such a prestigious center named in your honor?" she modestly said, smiling, "I am overwhelmed and humbled by the honor. In fact, I still cannot bring myself to answer the phone any way other than 'Arts Center.' I absolutely love every minute of every day of my life!" Patty's sweet spirit, charming personality, fierce determination and multitude of talents have enabled her to grow the Granville Arts Center into a facility that serves as a prototype across the Southwest. Our Lady's Day Out hats are off to Patty Granville, Garland's bright and shining star, who continues to bring down the house at the Arts Center named in her honor.

EBBY HALLIDAY

Her name is familiar to most every Dallasite; her "Sold" signs appear throughout the city; and her philanthropic involvement and contributions are legendary in Texas. Ebby Halliday is a remarkable businesswoman with an extraordinary success story.

Since its birth in 1945, Ebby Halliday Realtors has grown from one small office to 25 today, making it one of the largest and best-known privately owned residential real estate firms in the nation. It stands as No. 1 in the Dallas/Ft.Worth Metroplex, No.1 in Texas, and No. 20 in America, according to *REAL Trends, Inc.*

Ebby Halliday's life story has been peppered with trials and challenges, but also shines with great fortune and blessings. When asked how old she is, she will just grin, pat her immaculate snow-white hair, and tell you to "do the math." Ebby graduated from high school in 1929 in Abilene, Kan., just at the beginning of The Great Depression. Looking for a permanent job, Ebby took a job in the millinery department of the Jones Store in Kansas City earning $10 a week. She was transferred to Dallas, in 1938 to take a management position in the millinery department of W.A.Green Store, and found she really liked Texas. In fact, she liked it so much she decided to stay in the Lone Star state.

Her foray into the world of real estate came about through a doctor that removed her tonsils, Dr. McLauren. Ebby had saved $1,000 and wanted his advice about how to invest it. She says that Dr. McLauren was at first reluctant to advise her, stating, "I don't advise women. If they lose, they cry." Ebby certainly didn't cry when she turned that $1,000 into $12,000 by investing in cotton futures! That little nest egg enabled her to open her very own business—Ebby's Hats.

From hats to houses? That transition happened in 1945 when a developer approached Ebby with a challenge—to help him sell a development of post-war insulated cement houses. Ebby laughingly remembers, "They were very solidly built, but no one would buy them. They were not very attractive." He challenged her by saying, "If you can sell all those crazy hats to my wife, maybe you could sell my crazy houses!" Ebby did a little decorating—added carpeting, curtains, cottage furniture, and wall coverings, and sold every house within a year. That was it! Feisty, never-say-can't Ebby Halliday had successfully entered the real estate business.

Today, Ebby Halliday Realtors consists of more than 1,300 sales associates and over 200 employees, including 130 that are bilingual. Her services include home sales, in-house apartment and residential leasing, property management and even a counseling center to assist corporate transfers. For more than 60 years, Ebby Halliday has been helping families find homes in the Dallas area, with a sales volume of more than $3.8 billion in 2003. *Realtor Magazine* called her, "the icon for women in real estate" and "a role model for women entrepreneurs nationwide."

Her success has been phenomenal, but Ebby is most proud of the philanthropic work she has been able to fund because of her success. She gives much of her money and time to the community, and considers it a "must" for all of her associates to "give something back" to their community. Ebby's friends and business associates find it amazing that she can still maintain a full schedule of business and community engagements every day, (at 93, shhhh!), but Ebby is not one to sit in her office and sign checks. She wants to be personally involved, whether it is with a fund-raising luncheon, a client dinner or a special event. She has taken a special interest in the children's hospital, as well as education and the arts in Dallas.

Ebby has been successful in her business and her philanthropic work for many reasons. She has worked very hard through the years, treated her staff and clients with great respect, and understood the truth that the giver is always blessed. Ebby's incredible investments into Dallas will live on for generations. She has inspired many with her "bigger 'n Dallas" heart, and she's encouraged people to follow the directive of her late husband, Maurice Acers—"Do something for someone every day."

Do something for someone every day.

MAYOR LAURA MILLER

Before being elected to the Dallas City Council in 1998, Laura Miller was an award winning columnist and investigative reporter for the *Dallas Observer*, the *Dallas Times Herald*, the *New York Daily News*, the *Dallas Morning News* and the *Miami Herald*. She served three and one-half years as a member of the City Council representing Oak Cliff and Southwest Dallas before running for mayor, and was elected in February 2002.

Mayor Miller was born in Baltimore, Maryland, and is a graduate of the University of Wisconsin-Madison. She is married to State Representative Steven Wolens, who is a Dallas attorney, and they have two beautiful daughters, Alex and Lily, and a son Max.

One of the first items Mayor Miller tackled after her election was expediting the revitalization of downtown Dallas. She has also endeavored to improve the city's recycling program, reduce the crime rate, and with the help of her Faith Communities Coalition, buy out the flood-ridden Cadillac Heights neighborhood. She has worked tirelessly for affordable workforce housing, spearheading an unprecedented crackdown on unsafe, dilapidated apartment complexes. Her pressing commitment to making Dallas an internationally recognized destination city has involved projects to improve basic city services and beautify public parks. In fact, she views her greatest accomplishment to be the redesign of the Trinity River Project, which will include one of the world's largest urban hardwood forests, the creation of lakes, and a downtown riverfront park that, all totaled, will be 10 times larger than Central Park in New York City.

If you were to ask Mayor Miller about other things she considers her greatest achievements while in office, making Dallas a smoke-free city would rank among her top accomplishments. Under her leadership, the Dallas City Council enacted a citywide smoke-free policy that includes all indoor public spaces except bars, pool halls and tobacco shops. She hopes this measure will improve the health of Texans by reducing their exposure to secondhand smoke.

Mayor Laura Miller is an incredible woman. She is a wonderful wife and mother, a breast cancer survivor, and an energetic champion for the city of Dallas. Her political legacy includes programs that will benefit the city for generations to come. And, her go-getter attitude inspires the women of Dallas and beyond.

"I tell women to remember this: Whatever you want to do is completely attainable," Mayor Miller says. "People will tell you that you can't do it, that you don't have the money or connections or background to do it, but as long as you have confidence in yourself and passion, you can accomplish anything."

She is living proof of that. Who would have believed a woman from Maryland (known in Texas as a Yankee) could become mayor of Dallas? Yet, she has stepped into the position and made it her own, proving you don't have to be from Dallas to care about the city and her people.

Mayor Miller has helped define Dallas as an upbeat, business-like, get-it-done city with a future as bright as the Lone Star itself. We honor her as our first lady of Dallas.

LIZ MORGAN

Sometimes life throws "knuckle balls" that turn out to be "home runs," as evidenced by Liz Morgan's incredible and sweet success story. In 1989 a devastating experience left Liz responsible for supporting herself and her 15-year-old daughter. When faced with the challenge of making money, she immediately thought of the things she knew and loved the most—fashion, jewelry and people. She credits her mother for her "eye" for fashion and accessorizing. Her mother was a seamstress who sewed for many of the Dallas elite, and Liz learned from an early age the art of discerning not only fit but style. She started by going to the Dallas Market to purchase jewelry for friends. One day, she went to a hair salon where the customers literally bought the jewelry right off her neck! Liz said, "I marched right out to my car and brought in everything I had, and sold it all. That was my beginning."

At the time, she and her daughter lived in a tiny two-bedroom apartment. Money was tight, but Liz knew she needed to make a good impression with the vendors and her customers. So, in order to be able to buy from the major markets, she printed business cards to "look official," and began buying jewelry and accessories to sell—right from her living room! Friends began to tell other friends about Liz and the wonderful items she carried, and soon her small apartment was filled daily with customers. "Sometimes I had to move things off the bed to go to sleep at night!" Liz remembers. With a small amount of success, she and her daughter were able to buy a townhouse. They lived in the upstairs, and used the downstairs as a private store. This is what many of her longtime customers still remember and love. It was an intimate setting—cozy and welcoming —and they loved the special way they were treated when they came to Liz Morgan's home to shop. In fact, when she was finally able to open a "real" store, she had the building renovated and designed to resemble her old living room, and her customers appreciated that gesture. Today, they are as loyal as ever, and continue stopping by for browsing and visiting as they did in the early days. They can relax on the couch or enjoy a cup of coffee before shopping.

Several things happened in the course of Liz Morgan's rise to fame in Dallas that dramatically affected her success. One day, the marketing director for the Dallas Cowboys Cheerleaders came to her home to shop. She was responsible for a weekly publication that highlighted one of the cheerleaders in each issue, and Liz suggested that she could "dress them" with a unique style for the pictures. Of course, the girls wanted to buy everything she chose for them, and they began to tell their friends about the talented Liz Morgan. Talk about a divine appointment! Soon after, through the contacts of her brother and sister-in-law, Liz got the opportunity to be involved with the Miss Texas pageant and is still an integral part of this incredible event—another God connection that has made a difference for Liz.

Liz remembers fondly many of her previous customers, but especially the enchanting Mary Kay Ash, who shopped with her during the early days. In 1997, Liz moved her business to its present location at the Village on the Parkway, almost 10 years after the "hair salon" experience that inspired her to follow a dream. She continues doing all of the buying for the shop, and although she still goes to all of the major markets across the country, she says that Dallas is by far her favorite. There are very few women's specialty stores with the extraordinary inventory that Liz Morgan carries. She features both day and evening wear, and causal to runway, with lines such as Seven Jeans, Alberto Makali, Isabel de Pedro from Spain, Tadashi and Kay Unger. Women know when they shop Liz Morgan, they will find one-of-a-kind items they won't see in larger department stores.

In fact, Liz says she buys specifically with her loyal customers in mind. Her discerning eye for cutting-edge fashion coupled with her charming and friendly personality, have enabled Liz Morgan Womens Fine Apparel to become one of the city's finest treasures. Over the years, her clothes have graced the runways of numerous charitable fashion shows, many featuring Miss Texas contestants and the Dallas Cowboys Cheerleaders as models.

Liz Morgan has become a name synonymous with success and high fashion. Her clients include everyone from movie stars and high profile businesswomen to PTO moms and gals from the "hair salon." You will not find a harder working, more charming woman than Liz Morgan, and you will not find a place you love to shop more than her remarkable store. She has indeed come a long way from the two silver trays of jewelry she sold to friends and family to becoming one of the most respected and loved business women in Dallas, and she has certainly enjoyed the journey. Liz is honored that she has inspired so many people to turn their dreams into reality. "When you work hard enough, you can do anything you can dream," she says. "And, along the way you will find out just what you are made of. If I can do it, anyone can."

One step at a time, through hardships and tears to new friends and astounding blessings, Liz Morgan has made her incredible dream come true.

PAUL AND MARY BETH VINYARD
"BUBBA AND BABE!"

His baritone Texas drawl and her sweet southern smile are certainly two intangibles in the success story behind some of the South's Best Fried Chicken. Bubba's Cooks Country and Babe's Chicken Dinner House are said to "feed the soul of the South." Bubba and Babe are Paul and Mary Beth Vinyard, who along with their son Joel and daughter Tiffany Dawn have built a small empire of "chicken shacks" across northwest Texas. "Shucks," says, Paul, "It's just good country cookin'!"

Both Paul and Mary Beth grew up in a tiny Texas town called Turkey, which at that time boasted 900 citizens. (It has dwindled through the years to 350.) They have known each other since they were in sixth grade together, where Paul says, "She was taller than me then." Mary Beth Boswell's father was the Methodist minister in Turkey, so Paul treaded softly while courting his first love who would later become his bride. After high school, Paul attended Texas Tech University in Lubbock and Mary Beth attended McMurry University in Abilene. They then married and Paul began to work for large restaurant companies. By the way, he says that the marriage proposal came because of her delicious homemade yeast rolls. (Guess its true that the stomach is still the best way to a man's heart!)

Paul and Mary Beth grew up eating some of the "best food in the world," simple country cooking like fried chicken, chicken fried steak, fresh vegetables, flaky homemade desserts, butter biscuits and yeast rolls, and of course, lots of syrup and gravy "for dippin." "Why not bring this home-style, country cooking to others?" they thought. So, they opened their first restaurant, Bubba's Cooks Country in 1981 right in the heart of the posh neighborhoods of University Park and Highland Park where there was not a "Bubba" to be found. Paul and Mary Beth got a kick out of putting up their sign, because they lived in the surrounding neighborhood, and loved the irony of the name. Bubba's soon became the place to eat for SMU students, neighborhood families and businessmen. (There have even been a few famous Dallas Cowboys seen crunching down on a huge plate of fried chicken.)

With such incredible success at Bubba's, Paul and Mary Beth took the next step and opened the first Babe's Chicken Dinner House in Roanoke, Texas. Same great recipes, same down home atmosphere, same friendly folks to greet you at the door. All of the recipes used in both restaurants are ones that have been passed down for generations in both families. There's just one difference between Bubba's and Babe's—the food at Babe's is served family style. Heaping platters of meat, vegetables and bread are passed around as though you were eating in their home, and the sides are refilled until you can hardly push the chair back from the table. There are now Babe's restaurants in Garland, Sanger and Carrollton as well, and a fifth on the way in historic Burleson. Every one of the Vinyard restaurants is located in buildings that have some historical significance. The Dallas Bubba's is a restored Texaco station, and the Roanoke Babe's was once an old hardware store. Mary Beth has carefully created a warm, welcoming atmosphere that evokes memories of "grandma's kitchen" in each of their restaurants. Couple that with the unforgettable food, and it is no wonder that people just can't get enough of Bubba's and Babe's. In fact, when *Southern Living Magazine* polled readers about their "favorite" fried chicken the letters poured in by the hundreds. Two of the top-rated places for "finger-lick'n chicken" are none other than Babe's Chicken Dinner House and Bubba's Cooks Country!

Following in his father's footsteps, Joel Vinyard also got his business degree, and is now in training to one day take over the chain of restaurants. He is currently the floor manager in the Carrollton store. Daughter Tiffany has created and manages the catering for all of the restaurants. Paul says that she lives out of her pickup truck with her laptop, and is always on the go. Besides chicken, the delicious homemade pies are huge hits during the holidays. Cherry and Peach Cobblers and Chocolate, Coconut and Lemon Meringue Pies are so popular that lines form outside for pick up.

 The entire family works together every day in managing and growing this incredible group of restaurants. This wonderful stick-together, get-it-done, all-in-the-family attitude that has enabled the Vinyards to become so successful is exactly the spirit that permeates Dallas and indeed Texas. Dreams are big in the Lone Star state. The Vinyards followed their dream, put their hearts into the necessary hard work, and above all, have always treated their customers as friends. Bubba and Babe Vinyard are a delightful, hard-working couple who have created a legacy that will continue to "feed the soul of the South" with some of the best fried chicken in the world. (Sorry Mom.)

Discover Dallas

Perhaps the most sophisticated city in all of Texas, Dallas reigns as one of the top visitor destinations in the Lone Star state. Its topflight attractions, performing arts groups, world-class shopping and cultural diversity offer guests an intriguing blend of Southern hospitality and upscale entertainment. There is so much to discover in this "larger than life" city. The city's colorful history was shaped by cattle barons, bandits and outlaws, as well as business tycoons, football legends and fashion designers. Today, with a population of more than one million people, Dallas is growing at a faster rate than it has in any other decade.

Downtown Dallas

Downtown Dallas is an experience you will never forget. Its phenomenal towering skyscrapers and one-way streets can be a little intimidating, so the best way to enjoy downtown is to climb aboard a bus for a guided tour. You might begin at Dealey Plaza, where the city actually began, and see the Old Red Courthouse. Don't miss the Texas Cable News building and Belo building, where you can learn the rich heritage of Texas through historic wall murals. Right in the middle of downtown, you will find the Pioneer Cemetery, where many of the first families of Dallas are buried. The Dallas Area Rapid Transit (DART) light rail system is another great option for finding your way around the city. The rail trains travel in a 3.75-mile tunnel between downtown Dallas and Mockingbird Lane. It is located 60 to 120 feet under Central Expressway, and travels at speeds up to 65 miles per hour.

Of course, you will not be able to leave Dallas without a day at the Sixth Floor Museum at Dealey Plaza. It was here that alleged killer Lee Harvey Oswald fired the lethal shots that killed President John F. Kennedy November 22, 1963. A fascinating tour will take you on the motorcade route the president followed, and you can follow Oswald's steps through downtown and his taxi ride to the Oak Cliff boarding house. The tour also covers the Texas Theatre where Oswald was captured, and the basement where he was killed by Jack Ruby.

History buffs will also enjoy the "Legend of Bonnie & Clyde Tour," which uncovers the lives of the famous outlaw lovers from Dallas. Bonnie Parker and Clyde Barrow lived and worked in Dallas during the early Depression years. Clyde worked in a mirror shop on Swiss Avenue, and Bonnie worked as a waitress. You will see the location of an attempted ambush of the outlaws, as well as a safe house where a gunfight broke out between Bonnie and Clyde and the police. It ends with a visit to Barrow's Star Service Station and the final resting places of the two famous outlaws.

Dallas Favorites

You will find many wonderful and exciting things to do in Dallas, but visitors always seem to gravitate to a few of our favorites—shopping and eating! This is the absolute perfect city for both. When you hear that "everything is bigger in Dallas," that is especially true of the shopping opportunities. Whether you are looking for couture clothing from top world designers or western duds for a Texas Two Step, you will find it all. From rowdy to romantic, upscale cosmopolitan to rustic country, Dallas and the surrounding areas offer shoppers innumerable opportunities for wonderful quality and great bargains. One great way to enjoy shopping Dallas is to visit the many little "districts" that make up Dallas proper.

The Bishop Arts District, (B.A.D.) is a historic commercial area located at Seventh Avenue and Bishop Street. This area gained attention during the 1930s when it was the city's busiest trolley stop. It has undergone major restoration and renovation over the last 15 years, emerging once again as an eclectic collection of unique shops, restaurants and businesses. It is called the "hippest" shopping scene in Dallas and one of the hottest places in the city to see and be seen. The picturesque strip of old-time storefront buildings on

Bishop Avenue has been transformed into a funky, creative dining and shopping mecca, with period lighting reminiscent of the early days. You'll find art galleries, antique stores, gift boutiques and soda shops. Many of the restaurants have been touted as some of the best in Texas by nationally acclaimed magazines.

Uptown is a very "happening" place to shop in Dallas. A trolley from the Cityplace Subway Station in Uptown Underground connects Uptown visitors to the rest of city. Riders can hop off at any time to visit the many antique shops, art galleries and restaurants. Uptown is a fascinating area, well known for its eclectic atmosphere and wonderful shopping opportunities, but also for its contribution to the history of early Dallas. It is also known as the State Thomas Historic District, containing the most intact collection of historic residential structures of the late 1880s Victorian period in Dallas. A tour through Uptown reveals that eight Dallas mayors are buried here, two of which met untimely deaths in shootouts! This last remnant of a once fashionable, upper-middle class community is now an exciting little collection of wonderful shops and restaurants. You will love it!

Another commercial area near downtown Dallas that has maintained an historic 1920s ambiance is the popular *Greenville Avenue*. Located from downtown to Mockingbird Lane, Greenville Avenue attracts a young, professional crowd, with trendy restaurants ranging from casual to very elegant. The area comes alive each night as both locals and visitors flock to the unique shops, restaurants and hip clubs. The locals have divided the area into three sections. Upper Greenville is known for its cosmopolitan businesses, while Lower Greenville has unique, one-of-a-kind shops and outdoor dining sprinkled among quaint dwellings. Lowest Greenville, as you might imagine, is a free-spirited mix of homey pubs, ethnic restaurants and eclectic shops.

Deep Ellum – a trendy hip area just east of downtown Dallas has been described as "A Little New Orleans." This former warehouse district was once the hotbed of the "Blues" and African-American culture. The little bohemian village of Deep Ellum is now the Dallas headquarters for live music. You can explore the past, present and future of Deep Ellum and its music, and enjoy wonderful shopping and dining.

Historic Oak Cliff – It is called "The Hidden City," and is one of the greatest selections of historic homes in Dallas. The original Township of Oak Cliff dates to 1886 when it was platted as a residential community by Thomas Marsalis. By 1903 the community was annexed by the city of Dallas, but has endeavored through the century to remain a neighborhood with a unique atmosphere and character. Oak Cliff proper encompasses 20 venerable neighborhoods with residents as diverse as the architecture throughout the area. Rare Victorian homes of the original township, Prairie and Bungalow cottages are steeped in history, and are now being renovated and lovingly restored to their original beauty and charm. You will see history itself played out in the different styles of architecture, from the 1920s Tudor Revival and period style mansions to the 1940s and 1950s sprawling ranch-style homes.

One of the oldest houses in Dallas is located in the section of Oak Cliff called East Kessler. It is believed that construction on this house may have begun as early as 1851. It is called "The Rock Lodge," because the walls are actually four feet thick in some places, and was supposedly a stagecoach stop during the very early days.

The neighborhood of Lake Cliff probably contains more architectural history than any other place in Dallas. The man-made Lake Cliff was created in 1890, and is still considered one of the most beautiful parks in the city. The Depression years ended the long-time dream of Mr. Marsalis for Oak Cliff to be Dallas' most affluent suburb. He lost all of his business holdings, and his palatial 1889 residence sat unoccupied for many years before becoming the Marsalis Sanitarium in 1904. Unfortunately, the beautiful mansion was burned to the ground in 1915. Historians and conservationists believe that the Lake Cliff neighborhood of Oak Cliff offers one of the most historical and varied examples of architectural styles in all of Dallas.

The Oak Cliff area is blossoming with exciting new businesses and shopping centers including the revitalized Bishop Arts District, Jefferson Boulevard, Wynnewood Village, North Cliff Shopping Center and Southwest Center Mall. You will find everything from ethnic bakeries and bookstores to art galleries and wig shops. This historical oasis called Oak Cliff has grown to be one of the city's main tourist attractions and favorite shopping and dining experiences.

Highland Park–The area that is now home to some of the most exclusive homes and upscale businesses in the nation was first occupied by the remnants of a Texas Ranger scouting expedition in 1837. After a savage Indian battle, the rangers camped in a lovely spot on what they called "the creek with all the turtles." They were the first Anglo-Americans in the area known today as "Highland Park." In 1838, the Caddo Indian trail was surveyed by the Republic of Texas to become part of the National Central Road from the Red River to Austin. It was used then as a part of the Shawnee Trail for cattle drives to Missouri, and is known today as Preston Road. In 1843, Dr. John Cole of Virginia was the first person to acquire land in this area. He purchased the area that is now known as Highland Park and University Park. His son, Joseph Larkin Cole inherited this land in 1851, and sold it to Colonel Henry Exall between 1886 and 1889. Colonel Exall created Exall Lake, and began laying out the graveled streets, and raised trotting horses in this place he named "lomo alto," high land.

Mr. John S. Armstrong purchased the land in 1907 and began development of the residential community called Highland Park, which was incorporated in 1913. He envisioned an exclusive community just north of the busy and booming new city of Dallas. He hired Mr. Wilbur David Cook, the designer of the famous Beverly Hills community to lay out the town. Affluent citizens were drawn to the beautiful upscale area, and the Dallas Country Club was built.

The heart of town is called Downtown Highland Park, and is located between Mockingbird Lane and Preston Road. The Highland Park Village opened in 1931, but the completion of the Village as it is today took more than 20 years. The Village, as it is called, has a rather international flair. There are famous names like Hermes, Bottega Venata, Chanel and Escada, as well as wonderful little cafés and restaurants. During the holidays you will enjoy an annual Christmas Tree Lighting and Horse Drawn Carriage Rides.

Shop 'til you drop in the charming *Snider Plaza*. In 1926, C. W. Snider and J. Fred Smith purchased 30 acres of farmland from Frannie Daniels. They decided to develop a retail area and the first business opened in 1927. The last major building was constructed in 1947 and the character of the Plaza was complete. Located near Lovers Ln. and Hillcrest Ave., this is one of the best family-friendly spots in the Metroplex. Snider Plaza is home to dozens of charming boutiques and beloved dining spots from home cookin' to a more formal dining experience. Snider Plaza is like no other shopping community.

You must have sustenance to carry you through the matchless shopping excitement Dallas has to offer. Not to worry; Dallas boasts more than 7,000 restaurants and cafés, featuring everything from true Tex-Mex and pit-smoked barbecue to international gourmet cuisine and tearoom fare. In fact, Dallas has more restaurants per capita than New York City!

Dallas will indeed dazzle you, with her big-hearted Southwestern charm, unparalleled entertainment prospects and just the right touch of the "wild, Old West." We know that you will love exploring the different districts of Dallas, and discovering for yourself what makes this city a star that outshines all others. It does seem "larger than life," but will feel like home, thanks to the wonderful people who greet their visitors with warm Texas smiles and handshakes.

For more information about Dallas, contact the Dallas Convention and Visitors Bureau at 214-571-1000, 800-232-5527 or visit www.visitdallas.com online. Or, contact the Great Dallas Chamber of Commerce at 214-746-6600 or visit www.dallaschamber.org online.

Dallas Arboretum
8525 Garland Road • Dallas, TX 75218 • 214-515-6500

Dallas Children's Museum
13331 Preston Road Suite 308 • Dallas, TX 75240 • 972-386-6555

Dallas Museum of Art
1717 North Harwood • Dallas, TX 75201 • 214-922-1200

Fair Park Dallas
1300 Robert B. Cullum Blvd. At Grand • Dallas, TX 75210
214-670-8400

Farmer's Market
1010 S. Pearl Street • Dallas, TX 75201 • 214-939-2808

Meyerson Symphony
2301 Flora Street • Dallas, TX 75201 • 214-692-0203

Old City Park
1717 Gano St. • Dallas, TX 75215 • 214-428-5448

Science Place
1318 2nd Ave • Dallas, TX 75210 • 214-428-5555

Sixth Floor Museum at Dealey Plaza
411 Elm Street • Dallas, TX 75202-3308 • 214-747-6660

The Dallas Zoo
650 South R.L. Thornton Freeway • Dallas, TX 75203 • 214-670-6826

The Dallas Aquarium at Fair Park
1462 First Avenue & MLK Boulevard • Dallas, TX 75226
214-670-8443

The Women's Museum
3800 Parry Avenue • Dallas, TX 75226 • 214-915-0860

World Aquarium
1801 N. Griffin St. • Dallas, TX 75202 • 214-720-2224

The Dallas West End Historic District
Dallas Arts District
Slocum Street

Dallas Fairs Festivals & Fun

January
  Cotton Bowl in Fair Park
  Kid Film Festival
  Texas Home and Garden Show
  Winter Boat Show
  Winter Bridal Show

February
  Flower and Outdoor Living Show
  RV Show
  West End's Mardi Gras Parade
  Winter Boat Show

March
  Dallas Blooms at the Dallas Arboretum
  Spring Home and Garden Show
  St. Patrick's Day Parade
  World Golf Expo

April
  Dallas Blooms Spring at the Dallas Arboretum
  Folklorico Festival
  USA Film Festival

May
  Asian Festival
  Black Invitational Rodeo
  Cajun Fest
  Cinco de Mayo Celebration
  Safari Days at the Dallas Zoo

June
Summer at the Dallas Arboretum (Jun-Aug)

July
July 4th Celebration
Taste of Dallas

August
Elvis Run
Texas International Blues Festival
Woman's Expo

September
Freedom Run and Festival
Greek Food Festival
State Fair of Texas

October
American Indian Art Festival & Market
Boo at the Zoo
State Fair of Texas
Susan G. Koman Race for the Cure

November
Chi Omega Christmas Market
Holiday at the Arboretum
Turkey Trot

December
Candlelight at Old City Park
Jingle Bell Run
Neiman Marcus Adolphus Children's Christmas Parade

Antiques

LEGACY
Antiques and Fine Art, Ltd.

Jeff, Vicki and Justin Garrett welcome you to their magnificent antique showroom at 1406 Slocum St. in Dallas. The Garrett's are third generation family antique dealers and have been in the Dallas area for more than 30 years. Step inside and discover a vast array of fine 18th and 19th century European antiques and incredible works of art. You will find formal and country French furniture, Italian painted furnishings, Dutch furniture and selected Georgian articles from Britain. The 8,000 square foot showroom is filled with buffets, armoires, tables, bergeres, architectural pieces, marble fountains and more. We also loved the great selection of oil paintings, can-

delabras, beautiful clocks and a huge selection of breathtaking chandeliers. Legacy Antiques and Fine Art is open Monday - Friday 9 am - 5 pm and Saturday 10 am - 4 pm. Visit www.legacyantiques.com online or call 214-748-4606.

It has been described as an upscale flea market but think Paris or Portobello, because much of the merchandise arrives here from abroad. The Mews (mi uz) opened in Dallas during the summer of 1992, and has since become a favorite haunt of interior designers and professional antique dealers.

Owner Doris Hart gave the market the unusual moniker, which means "a stable of shops" or "a set of stabling grouped around an open yard or alley." Actually, the word "mews" is rooted in London. Around 600 years ago, it was the name of the royal stables at Charing Cross, which were built on the spot where the royal hawks were kept or "mewed." Whereas the idea of a collective market dates back to the Greeks, this marketplace meets the needs of today's shoppers who are looking for marvelous antiques, fine decorative collectibles and grand architecturals that are breathtaking.

There are approximately 90 dealers nestled in two brick buildings at the edge of the design district. And, much to the joy of the general public, The Mews is open to everyone. Dealers have brought together antiques and great decorative old pieces, elegant French furniture and one-of-a-kind accessories, making them available to all of us. Previously, such pieces were only available to designers with access to the market showrooms. The exceptional level of quality and taste represented here is unsurpassed in the southwest, and The Mews draws designers and buyers from New York to California.

The Mews is located at 1708 Market Center Blvd. and 1333 Oak Lawn Ave. and is open Monday-Friday 9 am - 5 pm and Saturday 10 am - 4 pm. For more information, call 214-748-9070, 214-748-8353 or visit www.themews.net online.

MCKINNEY AVE ANTIQUE MARKET

Treat yourself to a cup of coffee, and step "back in time" as you browse the incredible McKinney Ave Antique Market, 2710 McKinney Ave. It is located along the restored trolley line in the historic Dallas Uptown neighborhood, and its ambiance is warm and inviting. Brimming with treasures like vintage lace and linens, Staffordshire, Wedgwood, Chinese Export porcelain and majolica, The Market is a delight to explore. Under the ownership of Jane Dodge Howell, The Market continues to offer an eclectic mix of quality English, American, French and Oriental antique furniture and treasures, as well as vintage prints, oils, water colors, rare books and folk art. Shop Monday-Saturday 10 am - 5 pm and Sunday, October - June 1 - 5 pm. For more information, call 214-871-9803 or visit www.mckinneyantiques.com online.

WHITE ELEPHANT ANTIQUES WAREHOUSE

Kay Ross has been in the antiques business for more than 30 years, and she says, "the best way to describe our remarkable antiques warehouse is—Everything from Early Marriage to Veranda." The White Elephant Antiques Warehouse mall, 1026 N. Industrial Blvd. in Dallas, is 24,000 square feet of unbelievable merchandise at fantastic prices. Look for the long name on the front of the building between Howell and Payne Streets. You will find an incredible inventory of wonderful furniture, lamps, mirrors and a huge selection of rugs. Remember to look up at the more than 200 chandeliers! The Warehouse is open Monday-Saturday 10 am - 5 pm and Sunday 1 - 5 pm. For more information, please call 214-871-7966.

London Market

When you step through the door at London Market, you will feel as though you just walked into a London antique shop. The small select group of dealers, half of whom live in England, strive to provide an extensive selection of fine English furniture, collectibles and works of art for your shopping pleasure. They search the markets of England to find those unique pieces that will make you say, "That's just what I'm looking for."

Nell and Charles Roberts have been in the antique business for more than 25 years and have been importing containers of antiques from England since 1991. They take four trips a year to England, and for the last five years have been taking customers who want to tag along with them as they scour the markets and shops for special items.

They specialize in fine English furniture from the Georgian through the Edwardian period—with both formal and country pieces to fit your needs. They also carry a wonderful selection of large 19th century English and French mirrors—that you won't want to miss. You will love finding the best of the London markets without ever having to leave Dallas! Of course, a trip with Charles and Nell sounds like great fun too! Located at 5029 W. Lovers Ln., London Market is open Monday-Saturday 10 am-5 pm and Sunday 1-5 pm. For more information, visit www.londonmarketantiques.com online or call 469-335-9978.

Connie Williamson Antiques

She loves beautiful furnishings that go beyond functional, as well as extravagant accessories from exotic, distant places. "Always the Unusual" best describes this opulent antique store at 1080 Dragon St. in Dallas, where you will find an amazing collection of fine 18th and 19th century antiques and decorative accessories. Connie Williamson Antiques is open Monday-Friday 10 am-5 pm and Saturday until 4 pm. For more information, call 214-760-0100 or visit www.conniewilliamsonantiques.com online.

Artists, Art Galleries & Specialty Shops

In 1978 Wayne Lovell opened the doors to this Dallas neighborhood favorite, then known as "The Ole Moon & Other Tales: Preread Books & Other Friends." During its first decade, the shop was known for its extensive literary inventory, retro furnishings and funky jewelry. When managing partner and current director Rudi Riffkind joined the business in 1989, this already hip store was infused with an eclectic atmosphere, and the focus became "American contemporary craft items." The Ole Moon has earned local and national recognition for its outstanding selection of American-craft pieces such as estate jewelry, hand-blown glass, ceramic and wood pieces, and handmade greeting cards. In fact, well-known Texan Matthew McConnaghy dropped in to do some Christmas shopping, and proclaimed it "better than any place in New York or on Rodeo Drive!" Wow! Stop by 3016 Greenville Ave. and see for yourself! Open Tuesday - Friday 11 am - 7 pm, Saturday until 6 pm and Sunday noon - 5 pm. Call 214-827-9921.

Denny Doran credits his early days working on oil rigs, oil refineries and in factories, as much as his bachelor's degree from Notre Dame and his master's from Kansas University, in providing him with a lifetime of inspiration. He started drawing at 5 and painting at 8—always able to reveal beauty in the most mundane materials. When he met Katrina in 1992, he hired her as a model, married her in 1999, and now they reside and work at their multi-media Dallas studio at 110 Cole St. The building is one of the first tilt-wall construction buildings in the Trinity Industrial District and was built before WWII. Denny and Katrina produce oil and acrylic paintings of all sizes, abstract and representational—especially portraiture—sculptures, and mosaics. They welcome commissions in all these areas and guarantee customer satisfaction. For an appointment, call 214-748-4544.

SANDAGA MARKET AFRICAN IMPORTS

Sandaga Market African Imports sells indigenous art from the entire African continent. Owner Darryl Thomas provides authentic pieces used by Africans in their daily lives, specializing in items such as stools, tables, chairs and hand-woven textiles. He also carries fine hand-carved masks, instruments and shields, displaying them in unique settings throughout the gallery. From the unique bronze and wood sculpture of Central and West Africa to the small selection of rugs from Mauritania and the Middle East, you never know what treasure you will find at Sandaga Market. Located at 1325 Levee St. (at Cole) in Dallas. Stop by every "Second Sunday" for a fabulous Jazz concert in the showroom. Open Monday - Saturday 10:30 am - 6 pm. For more information, call 214-747-8431.

Bed & Breakfasts

The Corinthian Bed and Breakfast

Named for the beautiful fluted "Corinthian" columns that grace the front porch, this magnificent Dallas bed & breakfast inn offers guests the ultimate in luxury and comfort. Originally, the house was built for Dr. Garfield Hackler, Professor of Surgery at University of Dallas (Baylor Medical College) during the early 1900s. It was later owned by Sammie and Robert Franks, when it became known as "The Colonial, a Boarding House for Young Ladies." After Mrs. Franks' death at 92, Mr. Craig Penfold purchased the property, and restored the beautiful old home to its original splendor. The congenial staff's hospitality has made The Corinthian a premier Dallas inn.

Whether you are planning an overnight business trip, a romantic weekend, or a special party or reception, you will not find a more perfect place. The Corinthian exceeds every expectation for comfort, ambiance and romance. Every guestroom features king-size beds that are dressed in the most luxurious linens, private baths, telephone, TV, high-speed Internet and fresh flowers. You will wake to the aroma of freshly brewed coffee, which you can take into the Garden Room before enjoying a delicious gourmet breakfast. Each afternoon, guests will find an assortment of complimentary beverages, cookies and cakes—perfect for a quick pick-me-up after a day spent in the big city.

Consider The Corinthian when planning a wedding, reception or special occasion. The setting is incredibly beautiful, and there are planners to assist with all aspects of the event. This wonderful bed & breakfast is located at 4125 Junius St., just minutes from the center of downtown Dallas, and blocks from the Baylor Medical Center. For information or reservations, call 214-818-0400, 866-598-9988 or visit www.corinthianbandb.com online. *(Color photo featured in front section of book.)*

Books

Celebrating over 28 years in Snider Plaza, The Muse is one of Dallas' premier specialty shops. Ladies love The Muse! You'll find stationery, American and European greeting cards, as well as cards handcrafted by Texas artists. For an excellent selection of classic and contemporary books, gourmet foods, masks, music boxes, frames, friendship and fun all wrapped up in cozy, old-fashioned Victorian ambience, be sure to visit this wonderful bookstore and specialty shop, a true Texas treasure. *D Magazine* named The Muse one of the "Best Stores in Dallas" for 2003!

Artist owner Julia Murray decorates the shop for holidays and special events, provides complimentary hand-drawn gift bags with purchase, and you'll enjoy Julie's card line, "A Dachshund Looks at Life." The Muse is located at 6725 Snider Plaza in Dallas near Southern Methodist University. Open Monday-Saturday 10 am - 6 pm. Call 214-739-6011.

"Texas is a state of mind. Texas is an obsession. Above all, Texas is a nation in every sense of the word."

– Author John Steinbeck

Children's

BELLINI® When it comes to your baby you only want to give the best—Bellini offers just that. With its unique line of Italian-made furniture, Maclaren strollers and quality accessories, you'll rest easy knowing that your little one is safe, sound and stylish. If you need help designing the perfect nursery, Bellini's qualified staff can help. Shower Registry is also available. Bellini, 5600 Lovers Ln., #142, is open Monday - Saturday 10 am - 5:30 pm. Call 214-352-2512 or visit www.bellini.com online.

 the **wooden** swing **company** You'll find a variety of sturdy outdoor play equipment including forts and wooden swings, along with adorable bedroom furniture that your kids will love at The Wooden Swing Company. Family-owned-and-operated since 1978, The Wooden Swing Company is located at 13617 Inwood Rd., near The Galleria Mall in Dallas. Picture your kids playing on redwood backyard play structures by Backyard Adventures or sleeping in comfy beds decked out in quality bedding and accessories. That's what you'll find at this one-of-a-kind shop for children ages 2-12 years. Owner Royce Piper and her friendly sales staff will help you design a fun and functional backyard and a bedroom that's a special retreat for your child. Hours are 9 am - 5 pm Monday-Wednesday and Friday, 9 am - 7 pm Thursday and 10 am - 6 pm Saturday. For more information, call 972-386-6280 or visit www.woodenswing.com online.

Fashion, Accessories & Jewelry

ZOLA'S EVERYDAY VINTAGE

They share a love of beautiful clothing, all things vintage, and a grandmother named Zola Daffron. Cousins Annette Norman and Diedra Sutton have turned their love of collecting vintage clothing and accessories into a thriving business. Zola's Everyday Vintage is located at 414 N. Bishop Ave. in Dallas' Bishop Arts District. The window displays change every week and have become somewhat of a local attraction. You'll see colorful scarves, shoes, evening and cocktail dresses, vintage train cases, and costume jewelry, as well as a smattering of men's ties and shirts. The cousins also carry items by local artisans, giving them a special place to show off their talents. They also have a line of cards by artist Kay Peterson, featuring the shop cat "Sister!" Great shopping—great fun! The store is open Thursday 11 am - 7 pm, Friday-Saturday 10 am - 10 pm and Sunday 11 am - 4:30 pm. Call 214-943-6643.

Liz Morgan

womens fine apparel

Liz Morgan has come a long way since 1989 when her inventory only consisted of two trays of sterling silver jewelry. After a life-changing experience of becoming a single mom, Liz lived with her 15-year old daughter in a tiny Dallas apartment where she began buying and selling jewelry, coats, clothing and accessories. She says that, "The two silver trays expanded into enough merchandise to cover every inch of space in the apartment, and I had to move them off my bed to go to sleep!" Today, Liz Morgan Womens Fine Apparel is located in the Village on the Parkway, 5100 Beltline Rd., #800—the old Sakowitz Village. But some things never change. She had the 1500 square foot building renovated and remodeled to resemble her old living room, because she feels that retaining a feeling of intimacy with her customers has been a huge part of her success. Customers still feel as though they are visiting in her home. In fact, many sit and chat on the couch before shopping, or enjoy a cool drink of water or a cup of coffee at the bar.

The other secret to her success? Her inventory, of course. Liz Morgan is one of the very few women's specialty stores in Dallas, featuring casual, daytime and evening attire. She carries Albert Makali—exquisite suits and dresses, Isabel de Pedro—a line manufactured in Barcelona, Spain, and Anne Klein shoes.

Liz dresses many of the Miss Texas contestants and she is also the exclusive fashion coordinator for the Dallas Cowboys Cheerleaders, dressing them for calendar layouts, fashion shoots and personal appearances. Her beautiful shop has been featured in the *Dallas Business Journal*, *Women's Wear Daily* and in *"D" Magazine*. The store is open Monday-Saturday 10 am - 6 pm. Call 972-716-9446.

BEADS, BAGS N CHARMS

If you love jewelry—and who doesn't—we've found the perfect place for you—Beads, Bags N Charms, 11385 Harry Hines Blvd. This lovely store has a magnificent collection of beautiful and brilliant loose beads and gemstones. You'll find tables of loose beads and semi-precious stones displayed throughout the store, and the windows are decorated with beads, beads, beads of every color and shape.

Husband and wife Karim and Zabin Rajwani have created a unique and special store that caters to jewelry lovers of all ages. There is even a "99-cents wall" with trendy jewelry sets for teens and beginner beaders. Bring in a special idea and the Rajwanis will help you create the perfect piece of jewelry for any occasion. Many customers come in with a certain dress or outfit and design a one-of-a-kind piece of jewelry that finishes the look. After you have designed the perfect piece of jewelry for your special occasion, be sure to browse through the designer handbags, watches, sterling silver charms and luggage. The Rajwanis also carry many wonderful perfumes. The inventory is updated daily with the latest and most popular brands.

Zabin and Karim are always on-hand to make Beads, Bags N Charms your "one stop shop for all of your fashion needs." There are also bilingual assistants on staff to help Spanish-speaking customers. It is this kind of personal attention to every customer's needs that has earned the store a wonderful reputation throughout Dallas, and has made it extremely successful.

While in the area, be sure not to miss their other store—Beads N Bags—at 11022 Harry Hines. Beads, Bags N Charms is open Monday-Friday 9:30 am - 7 pm and Saturday 10 am - 7 pm. Visit www.beadsnbags.net online for a preview of some of their wonderful items, or call 972-241-6786 for more information.

J.R. & Co.

Whether you are shopping for yourself, own a small neighborhood boutique, or have a chain of retail shops, J.R. & Co. should be the first place you shop for the largest variety of fine jewelry, purses, luggage and fashion accessories. The entire Kim family works together in the shop and showroom, greeting each customer as a new friend. More than 80 percent of the business is wholesale, but retail customers are very welcome to shop the large inventory. You'll find fashion jewelry that would be stunning for an evening out, tiaras for proms,

weddings and quinceneras, and wonderful hair accessories. "Red Hat Society" ladies will be excited to learn that J.R. & Co. has an entire section just for them, featuring beautiful jewelry, pins, rings, scarves, earrings, necklaces and, of course, wonderful hats! The store is located at 11457 Harry Hines Blvd. in Dallas, and is open 8:30 am - 6 pm Monday-Saturday. Call 972-247-4577 or visit www.jrboutique.com online.

The Divas have created a remarkable little boutique featuring the latest in costume and fine jewelry, beautiful handbags and wonderful unique gifts. They are proud to be the only store in Dallas to carry Azarite™ jewelry—simulated diamonds set in 14-karat gold. You'll find semi-permanent lip color by Lip Sense and mineral based make-up by Colorescience. The store, located at 4412 E. Lovers Ln. is open Monday-Saturday 10 am - 5:30 pm. Call 214-696-6719.

Callidora

Callidora is a wonderful store filled with beautiful jewelry and unique home décor. It is located at 2913 Greenville Ave., in an area known for its many great restaurants and shops. Owner Roberta Campos's faithful customers know they will always find exquisite pieces of hand-beaded jewelry at very reasonable prices. She personally designs most of the jewelry and does custom work—sometimes even while you wait. So, if you can't find what

you're looking for on the shelves, Roberta will help you create the perfect piece to reflect your special style. You will love meeting the family—her husband Robert and their son Michael help out regularly. Even their daughter Hannah charms customers and helps mom "rearrange" the store! Callidora is open Tuesday - Saturday 11 am - 7 pm, Sunday noon - 5 pm. Call 214-515-9188 or visit www.callidoragifts.com online.

Today's mighty oak is just yesterday's nut that held its ground.

— Unknown

Florists

An old bicycle decorated with seashells and plants and the sound of wind chimes outside hint at the creative talent you will find inside Bishop Arts Floral—in the north Oak Cliff area of Dallas. This beautiful floral boutique is located at 412 N. Bishop Ave. in one of the original trolley stops of 1920 in the historic Bishop Arts District. Owners Don Allen and Phillip Wheless have been in the floral industry for more than 20 years. Don's love for floral design started when he was asked to help drive the delivery truck one Valentine's Day and the rest as they say is history! Don and Phillip have a distinctive floral style that is always in demand for weddings and special events. In addition to the fragrant fresh flowers and arrangements, you will find crystal suncatchers and metal crosses created by local artists, colorful lines of teapots, pet dishes and melodic wind chimes. You will simply love the magnificent floral topiaries filled with exotic and unusual flowers—we did! Open Monday-Thursday 9 am-5 pm and Friday-Saturday until 10 pm. For more information, call 214-941-8744, 800-834-2770 or visit www.bishopartsfloral.com.

dr. delphinium
DESIGNS & EVENTS

You'll love the beautiful, signature scent of fresh flowers when you walk through the door of this fantastic flower and gift shop at 5806 W. Lovers Ln. in Dallas. Dr. Delphinium Designs (we love the name!) was the first flower shop in the United States based on the European flower market concept. Consistently ranked by *D Magazine* as Dallas' best florist, Dr. Delphinium Designs was also named number one in a nationwide survey of 350 top national florists.

The high standard of quality and meticulous flower selection ensures only the freshest and most vibrant blooms are available, which results in longer lasting bouquets and floral arrangements. Dr. Delphinium Designs' weddings are elegant, romantic and memorable. With more than 20 years experience in catering, wedding planning and directing, the staff here will make your special day unique and unforgettable.

In fact, Dr. Delphinium Designs will make every occasion memorable, whether it is an arrangement for a small, intimate dinner party or a centerpiece for a large corporate event. You'll find everything from fresh cut stems and dried arrangements to plant baskets, orchid plants and collectibles. Of course, holidays are always bright and beautiful with unique arrangements for tabletops, mantels and banisters. So, let Dr. Delphinium Designs make your Christmas even merrier! The staff will even light your outdoor trees and shrubbery.

Dr. Delphinium Designs is open Monday-Friday 9 am -6:30 pm; until 6 pm on Saturday; and Sunday 11 am-5 pm. Call 214-522-9911 or visit www.drdelphinium.com online.

Furniture, Interiors & Value

Brother and sister Tracy and Honey Lanham opened this fabulous Dallas consignment store in 1989, and it has been a "family affair" ever since. When Honey retired in 2000, Tracy's wife Shari became his partner, and members from their big extended family help run the store. They have all been friends and family since 1940, and make a wonderful team. Customers say it's their favorite place to shop for wonderful antiques and home accessories, and they appreciate the great "consignment prices." The Consignment Collection, located at 12300 Inwood Rd., #116-A, specializes in antique furniture, china, crystal, collectibles and Victorian silver. Twice a year they do "Tablescapes" for a fall and spring charity event using items from the store. They have been featured in *The Dallas Morning News* and *Park Cities People*. Open Monday-Saturday 10 am - 6 pm. Visit www.consignment-collection.com online or call 972-788-4444.

SECONDS & SURPLUS
Building Materials

We love to find the most interesting places to shop, especially when they are stores that offer top quality at great prices. Seconds & Surplus, 909 Regal Row, is probably one of the most fascinating and exciting stores in Dallas. If you love saving money, you'll love this store! The showroom features the best value in the Metroplex on all home-remodeling materials. Owners Kevin Otto and Don Lett are able to buy discontinued, overruns, seconds and first-grade merchandise directly from the manufacturers at reduced prices and pass the savings on to their customers. Incredible as it may sound, the savings is generally 50 to 90 percent off retail!

The huge warehouse holds a large selection of oak and mahogany doors with decorative glass, kitchen cabinets and more than 50 styles of decorative cabinet hardware. There is a generous selection of laminate and hardwood flooring for every room in the house, and more than a million feet of decorative moulding. When you are ready for windows, you can select from 500 in-stock styles of either vinyl or aluminum. We also found the most beautiful fireplace mantels in a range of textures, styles and colors—each crafted with great classic detail. To complement the mantels, there are remarkable mantel clocks and a large selection of stand alone timepieces, all featuring traditional Westminster hourly chimes and toll.

Seconds & Surplus should be the first place you shop for all of your remodeling needs. The buyers search throughout the United States to find the highest quality merchandise for their customers, and sell lower than a national warehouse company. Call 214-637-3131 or visit www.secondsandsurplus.com online. Or, contact the Richardson store, 124 E. Arapaho, at 214-239-3131. Hours are Monday-Thursday 8 am-7 pm, Friday-Saturday until 6 pm and Sunday 11 am-5 pm.

The Consignment Store

A visit to The Consignment Store, 5290 Beltline Rd. in Dallas, is quite a "treasure hunt." You will be amazed and delighted at the incredible selection of beautiful new and gently used fine furniture, antiques, home accessories and market samples at very affordable prices. Open since 1986, The Consignment Store's unique blend of merchandise comes from the most beautiful homes and offices in the Dallas area. The furniture reflects both styles and colors that are currently in fashion. And, if it's gift items you need, there are crystal rose bowls, picture frames and porcelain vases just to name a few.

The Consignment Store's merchandise is added daily, so stop by often! The showroom is open Monday-Saturday 10 am-6 pm and Sunday noon-5 pm. For more information about this wonderful store, visit www.dallasconsign.com online or call 972-991-6268.

"If you've ever driven across Texas, you know how different one area of the state can be from another. Take El Paso. It looks as much like Dallas as I look like Jack Nicklaus."

— *Pro Golfer Lee Trevino*

Gifts, Home Décor, Bridal, Weddings & Specialty Shops

Suzanne and Mickey Roberts began their business in 1975 as "a way to make a little extra money." Today, this remarkable store is a much-loved mainstay at 6718 Snider Plaza in Dallas.

Specializing in fine gifts, stationery and tabletop accessories, Suzanne Roberts is one-stop shopping for brides. She carries a large selection of fine stationery for wedding invitations, birth announcements and party invitations. She is the only dealer in North Texas to carry the whimsical MacKenzie-Childs pottery and furniture. You'll also find the largest collection of Vietri Italian pottery in Dallas.

Order any of the many fine gifts from names like Spode, Halcyon Days, Jay Stronwater, Lady Primrose and Waterford at www.suzannerobertsgifts.com online. This beautiful store is open Monday - Saturday 10 am - 5 pm. Call 214-369-8336 or 800-266-0183.

HOLIDAY IDEAS
BY HAROLD F. HAND

Whether it is Halloween, Thanksgiving, Christmas, Easter, the Fourth of July or Mother's Day, Holiday Ideas overflows with decorative home accents and related gifts. It has been called, "a brilliant marriage of chic city pizzazz and country charm . . . with prices fit for perfect token trinkets or gifts of substance." Owner Harold F. Hand has been decorating the homes of friends and customers for years, and was finally persuaded to "hang out his shingle." The bright blue and yellow awning at the end of the Miracle Mile in Dallas acts as a shopping beacon for high quality, high sass and high fun. You'll find

beautiful items from Christopher Radko, Jay Strongwater and Dept. 56—everything from ornaments and wreaths to enameled boxes, clocks, candle holders and frames. Stop by Holiday Ideas, 4410 Lovers Ln., Monday-Saturday 10 am - 6 pm. Call 214-219-4332.

THE WRITE CHOICE

Jennie Malouf Gilchrist credits her father for her "editing eye." After working with him, she learned the art of "selecting the perfect mix" for her customers. The Write Choice, 4438 W. Lovers Ln. in

Dallas, is the only place to shop for stationery, invitations, photocards, engraving and gifts from baby to bride. Jennie's sweet, Christian spirit and the beautiful inventory make this store the absolute "Write Choice." Call 214-361-7012 to schedule an appointment or visit www.writechoiceonline.com.

Peek in the Attic

The quaint entryway to Peek in the Attic will take you back to the past as you catch a glimpse of Americana in the jewelry, seasonal items, candles and decorator plates just waiting to be discovered. You'll find pottery by Nickolas Mosse, bath products, Vera Bradley bags, specialty foods and much more—even rock candy brought in from Spain and vintage Christmas items!

Quality merchandise at moderate prices, coupled with friendly personal service, makes Peek in the Attic the place to shop for unique gift items, collectibles, specialty foods and so much more.

Peek in the Attic was founded in 1981 by Bill and Marsha Voinov and relocated to 6722 Snider Plaza in Dallas in 1988. Open Monday-Saturday 10 am - 5:30 pm. For more information, call 214-750-7335 or visit www.peekintheattic.com online.

Fête!
HOME COLLECTION

Located in the revitalized, historic Bishop Arts District, Fête! Home Collection is an eclectic home accessories boutique stocked with an array of furnishings not found in your run-of-the-mill retail shop. You'll find aromatic soy and ultra fragrant candles by Trapp, Tyler, Root and Voluspa, as well as unique furniture pieces that provide the perfect room accent. Original artworks from local artists line the walls, each with its own distinct personality. Fête! also features an abundance of items perfect for simple hostess gifts to the slightly more extravagant and hard-to-please recipient. Find Baudelaire and Niven soaps and lotions for your guests or yourself. Browse the character-filled vignettes for decorative chain pulls, hand-blown glass vases, embossed planters, greeting cards, jeweled pens, frog caches and more! Visit Fête!, 322 W. 7th St. at Bishop Ave. in Dallas. Open daily 11 am, call 214-948-9874 for additional information and closing times.

Talulah Belle

We can't begin to describe this wonderful store! It is delightfully unique and so much fun. You will find things here you've never thought about before, but all of a sudden can't live without! Talulah Belle, 2017 Abrams Pkwy. in Dallas, is the dream store of its owner, Elizabeth, who has an incredible gift for selecting "sassy," breathtaking treasures. From exclusive wedding gifts and home décor to Swarovsky Crystal pet collars and designer shoes—Talulah Belle has it all! Elizabeth also features an unforgettable, mesmerizing scent called "Child Perfume," which can only be found at limited boutiques throughout the country—it is almost addicting—as well as items such as Taylor bags, made-to-order Olivia Rose Tal shoes, and Lollia Boudoir Products. Visit Talulah Belle Sunday-Monday 10 am - 6 pm and Tuesday - Saturday until 8 pm. Call 214-821-1927 or visit www.talulahbelle.com online.

Pomegranates
The Party Place

Be sure and check out Pomegranates The Party Place of Dallas at 8411 Preston Rd. See page 209 for full details.

Lulu's Bridal Boutique

Be sure and check out Lulu's Bridal Boutique of Dallas at 2728 Routh St. See page 206 for full details.

So many cowboys, so little rope!

– Unknown

HOTEL **Crescent Court**

A ROSEWOOD HOTEL

DALLAS

If you want to escape to a world of fine linens, gourmet food, pampering beyond your wildest dreams and luxury at its finest, then hurry over to Hotel Crescent Court, A Rosewood Hotel, in Dallas. It's a tranquil island in the middle of a lively and exciting city.

This lovely hotel is the brainchild of Caroline Rose Hunt. More than 20 years ago, she opened The Mansion on Turtle Creek, which was the very first Rosewood Hotel. Her goal was to create an ambience of elegance without ostentation, an unrivaled level of personal service, and a beautiful expression of the surrounding area. She has achieved those aspirations with The Mansion on Turtle Creek, and with every Rosewood Hotel and Resort since, including Hotel Crescent Court.

In keeping with the Rosewood tradition of excellence, Hotel Crescent Court offers guests sophisticated, extravagant, uncompromising quality and legendary Texas charm. It was Caroline's goal to bring out the Texas charm, keeping with the company's mantra of "A Sense of Place."

Beautiful limestone walls envelop elegance, evident in every aspect of your stay—from the polished marble floors in the lobby to the goose-down duvet on your bed. All of the 220 rooms and suites feature French doors, plush bed linens, marble vanities, large custom desks and high-speed Internet. Nobu, the most innovative New Style Japanese restaurant in America, opens its doors at Hotel Crescent Court, in April 2005. Whether it's a special anniversary, a birthday celebration or a simple romantic overnight getaway, this place will serve up its finest for your special occasion.

Let's face it: no getaway is complete without a fabulous spa indulgence. So indulge away in one of 77 unique treatments offered at the world-renowned Spa at The Crescent. Whether you desire a spa pedicure, a spa manicure, a facial, a body wrap, waxing service, a body scrub, microdermabrasion or a special treatment bath, The Spa at The Crescent offers the perfect treatment specifically for your needs and wants.

Stop by this lovely hotel at 400 Crescent Court in the heart of the Uptown Arts District and experience life as it should be. It's not only a well-known hotel, it's a well-remembered one. Make some memories today. For reservations, call 800-654-6541, 214-871-3200 or visit www.crescentcourt.com online. *(Color photo featured in front section of book.)*

Museums

Thousands of men, women and children have been transformed by the knowledge gained at The Women's Museum in Dallas. Interactive exhibits and innovative programs showcase the accomplishments and achievements of American women through history. The Women's Museum is located at Fair Park, and is a National Historic Landmark. Visitors learn about more than 3,000 inspiring American women who have helped shape Texas, our country and our world. The "Wall of Words" greets visitors to the Museum. It is filled with visual and interactive exhibits that explore the lives and contributions of extraordinary women through the years. Women in the fields of art, sports, health care, business, technology, television, radio and religion are spotlighted. Be sure to visit the Museum Store, which offers a wide selection of apparel, cards and books. The Women's Museum is located at 3800 Parry Ave. and is open Tuesday-Sunday noon-5 pm. For more information, call 214-915-0860 or visit www.thewomensmuseum.org online.

OLD CITY PARK

The Historical Village of Dallas

A group of history-minded women convinced the city of Dallas in 1960 to move the 1861 mansion "Millermore" from Oak Cliff. It was the first of more than three dozen buildings to be relocated to what is now known as "Old City Park" near downtown. It is the city's only living history museum. Visitors are immersed in an experience unlike no other in North Texas, where living history characters recreate a typical day in early Dallas. Tour elegant Victorian homes, a school, a church and turn-of-the-century commercial buildings. "We want people not only to learn about history," Curator Hal Simon says, "but to see, touch, hear, and even smell what life was like in Dallas more than a century ago."

Interpreters portray Dallasites of 1861 and 1901, as they would have lived during that time. On one side of the museum, animal skins hang on the wall of the 1861 farmstead, and a village potter crafts stoneware using a foot-powered kickwheel. Donkeys Nip and Tuck are hitched to a wagon that will carry you on a ride through the museum. Walk to the other side of the museum, and you have skipped ahead to 1901, a time of economic growth and social change in Dallas, fueled by the railroads. See Victorian homes, a bank, a dentist's office, a print shop, a lawyer's office and a saloon.

"Candlelight at Old City Park" is an incredible experience during the holiday season with traditional music, lovely dancing, children's activities and beautiful lighting. The historic structures and grounds are also available for weddings, receptions and corporate functions. For information or reservations, call 214-413-3669 and be sure to visit www.oldcitypark.org online. Old City Park is located at 1717 Gano St., and is open Tuesday-Saturday 10 am-4 pm and Sunday noon-4 pm. This should be a priority when planning your trip to Dallas! It is an incredible experience.

Quilts, Needlework & Stitchery

Jackie Merriman's enjoyment of people and her work show through each beautifully stitched item displayed at Yarn and Stitches, 15615 Coit Rd., #206. This favorite Dallas specialty shop is filled top to bottom with yarn and stitching supplies, and you will usually find a group of laughing "stitchers" around a table finishing a project or two. Weekly classes draw people from as far away as Corsicana. Jackie also supplies yarn to the Women's Federal Prison in Ft. Worth, where knitted items are turned back into the DFW area to help those in need. The store is open Monday-Wednesday 10 am-5 pm, Thursday noon-8 pm, and Friday-Saturday 10 am-4 pm. Call 972-239-9665 or visit www.yarnandstitches.com online.

Restaurants & Tearooms

Reflecting the rich and rustic flavor of El Salvador, as well as the spicy, colorful comfort of local Tex-Mex, Gloria's Restaurant serves up authentic, delicious dishes from personal family recipes. Jose Fuentes tops off his incredible menu with a lineup of 37 varieties of tasty margaritas that go well with the cuisine that has been dubbed "Salva-Mex." Choose an entrée that is totally Salvadorian like Pescado Acajutia—tender marinated Tilapia fish served with gallo pinto and guacamole salad. Or, try something familiar and tasty like Enchiladas Verdes. The Fuentes family has opened Gloria's Restaurants—named for Jose's wife—in six locations, and promises that your visit to each will be extremely memorable. Visit the three Dallas locations at 600 W. Davis S., 3715 Greenville Ave. and 4140 Lemmon Ave. #102. Or, stop by Gloria's other locations: 8600 Gaylord Parkway #5 in Frisco, 5100 Beltline Rd. in Addison, and 5611 Colleyville Blvd. #300 in Colleyville. The restaurants are open daily 11 am - 10 pm and Friday and Saturday until 11 pm. For more information, call 214-948-3672.

Fried chicken says "Southern" like no other food, and Southerners take their fried chicken very seriously. In fact, when *Southern Living Magazine* polled readers about their "favorite" the letters poured in by the hundreds. Two of the top-rated places for "finger-lick'n chicken" are right here in the Dallas area, and we've tried them both! Coincidentally, they are owned by the same family and share the same secret Vinyard family recipes.

Bubba's Cooks Country is located in the upscale University Park neighborhood in Dallas, just across the way from Southern Methodist University at 6617 Hillcrest. Bubba's is located in a converted 1920s Texaco station—in fact, the men's room is still outside to the back of the building and the kitchen and serving counter were once the old service bays! The gas station turned chicken shack has been a Dallas landmark for more than 24 years. Mary Beth and Paul Vinyard chose the name "Bubba's" because the name was so completely opposite the very sophisticated business names nearby.

These two warm-hearted Southern souls grew up on West Texas homemade, country food and wanted to duplicate those same dishes in their restaurants. Why not start your day at Bubba's with a full breakfast, complete with homemade cinnamon rolls, muffins and buttermilk biscuits. Then, return for lunch or dinner. The menu is simple: fried chicken, chicken fried steak, fried chicken fingers, grilled chicken fingers and fried catfish. Each entree is prepared in small batches, and is served piping hot with sides of buttery mashed potatoes and cream gravy, green beans, coleslaw, baked beans and fruit salad. Of course, no Southern dinner would be complete without rolls, and Bubba's homemade yeast rolls will melt in your mouth. You'll also find sorghum and Texas Hill Country honey on each table. Just when you think it couldn't get better, they bring out the best for last—homemade Banana Pudding, just like Mom used to make. You are in for such a treat when you visit Bubba's "Cooks Country," 6617 Hillcrest; open daily 6:30 am-10 pm. And, don't forget to stop by their other fine restaurants: Babe's Chicken Dinner

House. There are four locations throughout the Metroplex. Call 214-373-6527 for more information. (See pages 78 & 232) *(Color photo featured in front section of book.)*

Cretia's joy and passion for baking, her contagious smile, her love of people, and her innate retail savvy have resulted in one of the most popular and fun places to dine and shop in Dallas. Cretia's on McKinney is an intoxicating blend of Bistro, Bakery, Bar and Clothing. Located at 4438 McKinney Ave., you can enjoy an incredible menu of perfect salads, warm sandwiches and pastas, as well as dinner items such as Pecan Crusted Catfish, Seared Pepper Crusted Pork Tenderloin and Fried Green Tomato Lasagna. And, don't miss out on the spectacular Sunday brunch.

Also, be sure to visit Cretia's Tea Room, located at 215 W. Camp Wisdom Rd. in Duncanville, which not only specializes in homemade goodies such as cakes, pies and cookies, but also offers scrumptious lunches, beautiful flowers and a warm ambiance. Last but not least, stop by the upscale, fun, ladies clothing boutique, adjacent to the Tea Room, which specializes in the hottest fashion trends.

The winning combination of great food, fashion and gifts, as well as the staff's warmth and friendliness will ensure an incredible experience that you won't soon forget. For more information and hours, call 214-252-9300 or visit www.cretias.com online.

In a fast paced world such as ours, the friendly folks at Short Stop Food To Go, 6918 Snider Plaza in Dallas, make life just a bit easier. This popular little neighborhood gem is a lifesaver for on-the-go students, soccer moms or career people who don't have time to spend slaving over a stove. Janis Estrada serves up delicious sandwiches, soups and salads, as well as appetizers, "ready to heat" entrees, and of course, delectable sweets for every occasion. Stop in Monday-Friday from 8 am - 6 pm or Saturday 9:30 am - 2:30 pm. Try our favorite—corn relish dip served with Fritos, as well as rice artichoke salad and spinach chicken enchiladas. Sweets include praline thumbprint cookies, cheesecake brownies, and tart lemon squares. Short Stop Food To Go is located near SMU in the quaint Park Cities neighborhood. Customers have learned to love and depend on this wonderful little place. Call 214-360-0311.

Angela's Cafe

From the spectacular breakfast specialties (like delicious Migas) to lunch and dinner favorites (like chicken fried steak and homemade fresh fruit empanades), you'll love everything on the menu at Angela's Café in Dallas. Located at 7979 Inwood Rd. in Dallas at the corner of Inwood and Lover's Ln., Angela's is a favorite with Park Cities' residents and visitors alike. The home-cooked dishes include Mexican, New York deli and, of course, great Southern dishes. With the support of the entire family, owners Anna and Angel Rodriguez opened the café in 1999. It became so popular, they had to relocate to this larger space in only two years. The atmosphere is casual and fun, with groups of lunching ladies, businessmen, and tourists enjoying the fresh-from-the-oven specialties. Angela's Café is open Monday-Friday 6 am - 9 pm; Saturday until 8 pm; and Sunday 7am - 3 pm. Call 214-904-8150.

 **De Tapas**
Restaurant

Owners Carlos Lukie and Joe Moreno welcome you to visit De Tapas Restaurant and taste the delicious Spanish family recipes prepared by mother-in-law/chef Carmen Jimenez. They invite you to relax to the soft tones of the Spanish/Latin music of Rumbaleo and to enjoy a glass of homemade Sangria. Located at 5100 Belt Line Rd., #764, near the Dallas N. Tollway, De Tapas is open Tuesday-Sunday. For more information and hours, call 972-233-8553 or visit www.detapasrestaurant.com.

Be sure and check out Mama's Daughters' Diners in Dallas at 2610 Royal Ln. and 2014 Irving Blvd.. See page 172 for full details.

Just so you'll know . . .
Dallas has more restaurants per
capita than even New York City.

Salons, Spas & Indulgence

THE *Spa* AT THE *Crescent*

DALLAS

ROSEWOOD HOTELS & RESORTS

Want to get away for a day? Feel the need to pamper yourself? Then, The Spa at The Crescent, 400 Crescent Court, is perfect for you. This world-renowned spa is committed to helping its clients reach a higher level of health, beauty and well-being. Therapists perform more than 77 treatments inspired by ancient traditions from around the world. With 22,000 square feet, The Spa at The Crescent offers 16 state-of-the-art treatment rooms. Not only is The Spa beautiful, the staff is very knowledgeable and skilled. Whether you want a spa pedicure, a spa manicure, a facial, a body wrap, waxing service, a body scrub, microdermabrasion or a special treatment bath, The Spa at The Crescent, Dallas has got you covered.

When Caroline Rose Hunt created her first Rosewood Hotel by transforming an old Dallas mansion into a world-class restaurant and hotel, she aspired to do three things: offer an ambiance of elegance without ostentation, an unrivaled level of personal service and attention to detail, and a beautiful expression of its location. When she gave birth to Hotel Crescent Court, she continued to follow those aspirations, knowing that this property had to have a world-class spa as part of its overall offerings. Thus, The Spa at The Crescent was born.

It's simply a spa to be experienced like a glass of fine wine. Relieve stress with a calming aromatherapy treatment or experience heaven on earth with one of the many extraordinary massages. From Swedish to Thai, Deep Tissue to Hotter 'n Texas Summer Rock Massage, you will find one suited to your specific needs and desires.

If you want to firm up those buns and work on your six-pack abs, The Spa has something for you, too. Professional trainers offer classes in strength building, aerobics, cycling, yoga and Pilates, and the fitness equipment is absolutely the best of the best. You'll receive instruction from top-notch fitness professionals in an environment that is inspiring.

No visit would be complete without spending some time and money in The Spa Boutique. There you'll discover the world's most advanced skin and beauty formulas, as well as wonderful gift items. Don't forget to ask about special packages. There are many to choose from, including: the Ultimate Bridal Package, the Rejuvenation Package, the Indulgence Package, the Body Contouring Package, the Vinotherapy Package, the Girl's Hideaway Package and more! For more information, visit www.crescentcourt.com online, or call 214-871-3232 or 800-828-4772. *(Color photo featured in front section of book.)*

In a hectic world where everything takes place at what seems to be the speed of light, the stress of the outside world can take its toll on our bodies. Sharon Medina and her highly trained staff at Face & Body Spas in Dallas and Frisco invite you to arouse your senses and awaken your spirit. The experience begins the moment you walk through the doors and hear the "other world" sound of water, music and chimes. It sets the tone for your journey. You will be cocooned in plush blankets and treated to a fragrant cup of herbal tea—Ginger Peach is a favorite flavor. As your therapist begins to nurture your skin and body, you feel as though you are "surrendering your reality."

Skincare therapists provide luxurious, results-oriented facials and expert waxing. Try one of their Age Defiance Facials and see an immediate difference in your skin. Massage therapists offer a full range of treatments including LaStone™, Swedish, pregnancy, therapeutic and Reflexology. Shed your tired skin with a fragrant honey almond, chocolate or citrus sugar body scrub. And don't leave without having a nail therapist exfoliate and massage your hands and feet. As all good things must come to an end, leave with the perfect OPI color on your nails.

Sharon carries professional skincare lines, including Babor, MD Skincare, Dermalogica, and Skinceuticals. You will also find for-home-use products, such as exfoliating gloves, aromatherapy lotions, and the fragranced salt and sugar based products. The retail area features blankets, robes, herbal tea, candles and books that allow you to create your own "home spa experience."

Located at 18800 Preston Rd. in Dallas and 1549 Legacy Drive in Frisco, the spas have gained the reputation for excellence, being featured in *Spa Magazine* and named one of 2004s "Best Day Spas" in Dallas by *D Magazine*. Come experience luxury at its finest at either location. Both Spas are open Monday - Saturday 9 am - 7 pm and the Frisco location is open Sunday from 9 am - 4 pm. Call 972-599-0881 (Dallas) or 972-668-6108 (Frisco) for an appointment. To learn more, or to shop online for those hard-to-find spa products, visit www.FaceandBodySpas.com. Look for a third location to open in Fall 2005.

Transportation Services, LLC

Premier Transportation Services, 7777 Lemmon Ave., Suite #100, is one of the largest providers of chauffeur-driven transportation services in the Dallas/Fort Worth and North Texas area. Providing transportation in all major cities of the United States, Premier has affiliates throughout the world. Its top-flight fleet consists of luxury Lincoln Towncars, executive corporate vans, 10-passenger stretch limousines, SUVs, Limo Buses, and mini and coach buses. Premier offers airport transfer service, wedding transport, large group transportation, and great nights out on the town! The limo drivers are professionally trained and licensed, guaranteeing the most reliable, safe and pleasant experience. Leave the details to Premier Transportation Services; sit back and enjoy the ride! Always available daily for reservations or information, call 214-351-7000, 800-789-4847 or visit online at www.premierofdallas.com.

Discover Carrollton

Historical Carrollton

Carrollton is one of three communities in the crest of the Dallas metropolitan area that has been named the "Metrocrest." Collectively, the Metrocrest includes more than 50 square miles, supporting a dynamic business and industry base, with almost 2,000 acres of parks, lakes and cultural entertainment centers.

Historians believe that Carrollton was named for the settlers who migrated here from Carrollton, Ill. The town was officially named in 1878 when the first U.S. Post Office opened, but the earliest settlers found this area as early as 1840. Many stories have been handed down through the years about Carrollton's early days, but the history books say the first settlers here were farmers, teachers, lawyers, preachers and doctors. For the most part, the new settlers were camping and building cabins in the present day Perry Park area because the high elevation of the land was a good "lookout," and the springs provided plenty of good water. Carrollton was once home to the Wichita Indians, who were eventually threatened by the Comanche, causing them to move to Oklahoma. The A.W. Perry Cemetery at Sherwood Dr. and Perry Rd. is the site of 482 graves of many of the earliest pioneers, and Pioneer Park (near Carrollton's first City Hall) is a half-acre mini-park dedicated to the families who settled this area.

During the early 1900s when "cotton was king," there were as many as 13 cotton gins in the Carrollton area. In 1904; however, a new industry emerged in Carrollton—manufacturing brick. The Carrollton Pressed Brick Company was built adjacent to the

Cottonbelt and Frisco railroads, just northeast of the Carrollton Town Square. In fact, the "Carrollton" bricks were used in the construction of many of the town's historic homes and buildings.

With the coming of the railroads during the 1800s, Carrollton developed into a large shipping location for cattle and became a town bustling with commerce and professional activity. By 1908, there were several railroads using Carrollton as a station—the Dallas-Wichita, the Cottonbelt, the Katy, and the Frisco Railroad. The tracks of three of these railroads intersect what is now the Carrollton Town Square. The charming gazebo that graces the middle of the Town Square is still used today by political candidates and town bands, as well as for theatrical entertainment.

Carrollton Today

With a population of more than 115,300, 5,200 businesses and a wonderful prime location, Carrollton has been called a city with a "home advantage." Just minutes from downtown Dallas, and a little more than 10 miles from DFW International and Love Airports, Carrollton is close to many regional attractions and professional sporting events. It has also been called a "Kid Friendly City," "Tree City USA," and "Texas' Safest City." Award-winning sports complexes, libraries, natural areas, golf course and beautiful municipal areas enhance Carrollton's diversity, making it a vibrant corporate and residential community.

In describing Carrollton today, you might say that it "exudes early 20th century charm." The Town Square has been infused with life. A charming gazebo is usually filled with both locals and visitors gathering to enjoy an ice cream cone, peek into one another's shopping bags, or just catch up on the town news. Delightful restaurants, wonderful antique shops and unique little boutiques will keep you busy for quite a while; then grab a park bench and enjoy a sweet moment of nostalgia. All of this is secretly nestled just one block off I-35. Most who take this daily drive up and down this passage have yet to discover the quaint but jazzy Town Square Carrollton has to offer. We loved it! *(Color photo featured in front section of book.)*

For more information about Carrollton, contact the Metrocrest Chamber of Commerce at 972-416-6600 or visit www.metrocrestchamber.com online.

Carrollton
Fairs Festivals & Fun

January
Pool Trout Fish-Out

February
Sweetheart's Ball

March
Sandy Lake Fun Fest (March-May)

April
Elm Fork Nature Fest
Old Downtown Shop-to-Shop Hop
R. L. Turner Torch Run

May
Mother's Day Concert

June
Battle of the Brains

July
Celebration Fireworks Show
Old Downtown Red, White and Rock 'n Roll

August
Teen Back to School Bash

September
Old Downtown Merchant's Inside/Out Sale

October
Halloween Carnival
Carrollton Country Fair

November
Old Downtown Holiday Open House

December
Old Downtown Holiday Parade and Tree Lighting
Old Downtown Santa on the Square
Old-Fashioned Christmas

The Finishing Touch Antique Mall

We know where you can find the perfect "finishing touch" for your home! You'll experience a journey into yesteryear when you visit this wonderful antique mall, The Finishing Touch, at 1109 S. Broadway in Old Downtown Carrollton. You'll find more than 30 dealers under one roof with marvelous selections of antique furniture, brilliant glassware, estate silver, kitchen collectibles, linens and quilts. Discover room after room of large European and American antiques, primitives, architectural pieces and rare collectibles. And you'll find the

perfect "finishing touch" for every room in your home! Owners Carol and Richard Fleming invite you to visit Monday - Friday 10 am - 5 pm, until 5:30 pm on Saturday and Sunday 1 - 5 pm. For more information, call 972-446-3038.

Past Times Antiques

Located in Old Downtown Carrollton at 1013 S. Broadway, Past Times Antiques is packed with fine furniture and collectibles. Specializing in kitchen items from enamelware to Depression glass—there is much to see in this special store. Owner Barbara Dean carefully selects the shop's glassware, porcelain, linens, lamps and dinnerware, along with hard-to-find items including salts and salt spoons. This is the place to go for vintage furniture: tables, buffets, armoires, blanket boxes and curio cabinets.

Past Times Antiques is open 10:30 am-4:30 pm Tuesday-Friday and Saturday 10 am-5 pm. Call 972-245-5416.

𝒫laza Arts Center

Don't miss this touch of creative genius in Old Downtown Carrollton! The historical Plaza Theater has been transformed into an art lover's paradise, where fine art and history blend together to draw you into a showcase of award-winning works in oils, pastels, charcoal, pottery, blown glass, sculpture and photography. A historical landmark in Carrollton since 1949, the building that once housed a movie theater now offers art classes, monthly events, onsite demonstrations by artists, and a chance to purchase a few pieces of art to add to your collection. And, if you are looking for a "special" loca-

tion for a "special" event, this is the perfect place! Located at 1115 Fourth St., Plaza Arts Center is open 10 am - 6 pm Tuesday through Saturday and 1 pm - 5 pm on Sunday. Call 972-242-6453 or 972-446-3200.

Fashion & Accessories

a Honey of a Deal and Company

If you are looking for casual work and weekend clothes—French Dressing Jeans, Cactus Flower—and you are a Missy or Plus fit, then Paula and Ann have the clothes for you! They even design their own line of separates. Come and find a terrific selection of decorative and useful gifts, wonderful cards, lotions and more. You'll love Ruby Lips, Sarah's Angels, Hot Flash Fannies and Artwear Reading Glasses.

Located in Carrollton's historic Town Square, A Honey of A Deal, 1106 W. Main St., is open Monday-Friday 10:30 am - 6 pm and Saturday 10 am - 5 pm. For further information, call 972-446-5654.

Gifts & Home Décor

Entering this charming, historic, 100-year-old "ginger-bread" house is like stepping back in time. Instantly, you will be greeted with delightful scents from Tyler, Archipelago, Lampe Berger and other purveyors of fragrance. Your eyes will dance with the feast of unique gifts and home accessories—especially the selection of beautiful and affordable lamps. Ready to pamper yourself? Lady Primrose, Thymes and Camille Beckman to the rescue! Maybe travel is "your bag?" Check out the Vera Bradley and Glen Royal Chic bags and travel accessories. As an award-winning retailer of Tracy Porter products, you'll find a wide selection of these enchanting items throughout the store. The Vintage House, 1101 Beltline Rd. in Carrollton, is open Monday-Saturday 10 am-6 pm. Call 972-242-5616.

Silver ★ Star

Antiques & Gifts

More than a specialty gift and home décor shop—Silver Star is family tradition, Texas pride and true Southern hospitality at its best! Located at 1102 W. Main St. on Old Downtown Carrollton's historical square, Silver Star is as original as the exposed ceiling tiles in the beautiful old building and as colorful as its barn-red floors. The shop is named after owner Susan Myers' family ranch called, "Silver Star Ranch." Husband Raymond grew up in Carrollton where his father owned a store in this section of town for many years. In fact, the Myers were one of the founding families of Carrollton. When this space became available, it was a dream come true and confirmation that it was "meant to be."

When Susan and Raymond renovated the building, their desire was to take it back to its original structure and design. The shop is filled top to bottom with wonderful American primitives, original art, Texas-made furniture, vintage jewelry and candles. And, the colorful, patriotic Texas and USA theme that permeates the store is warm and welcoming.

Susan and her forever friend Jackie have traveled throughout the country over the years and collected an amazing selection of unique antiques and primitives. You're going to love this store! The owners are friendly and vivacious people who absolutely love their business and the opportunity to share their stories with others. In fact, many of the items you'll find in the store are one-of-a-kind gifts from talented American artists. The Silver Star is open Tuesday-Saturday 10 am - 6 pm. You can contact Susan at 972-242-4490.

Ten of Arts

Ten of Arts—an unusual name for a wonderful gift shop! Owners Pat Malone and Lynne Hosid have transformed the original 10-artist gallery—thus the darling name—into an important downtown destination. They strive to present unusual and unique items to their customers, from wonderful Trapp candles and jewelry to home accessories and seasonal decorations all beautifully displayed with a sprinkling of antiques and collectibles.

Ten of Arts, 1105 S. Broadway in Carrollton, is open Monday-Saturday 10:30 am-5 pm. For more information, call 972-242-3357.

Mary Lou's
Gifts & Collectibles

After 20 years in business, owner Mary Lou Powell knows the value of quality customer service. That's why her store, Mary Lou's, is known as "the friendly shop." You will find boutique clothing, home décor, jewelry, collectibles, antiques and specialty items like Byers Choice, Fenton Art Glass, Willow Tree Angels and Boyds Bears as well as individual service.

Mary Lou's, 1017 S. Broadway in historic downtown Carrollton, is open 10:30 am - 5:30 pm Monday-Saturday. Call 972-466-1460.

Quilts, Needlework, Stitchery & Specialty Shops

When you're searching for that perfect present, you want to give something that is as special as the person receiving it. It needs to be a treasure, and at Softwear Embroidery you're sure to find just that. You can choose from a selection of new baby gifts, unique "Grandma" shirts, monogrammed linens and so much more.

Owner Lorraine Putney, who first began her business in her Minnesota basement, now puts her talents to work creating personal gifts for the whole family. Softwear Embroidery will make your gift giving memorable.

Softwear Embroidery, 1014 S. Broadway #104 in Old Downtown Carrollton, is open 10 am-5 pm Tuesday-Friday and 10 am-4 pm on Saturday. Call 972-245-2994.

The Old Craft Store

The old Carrollton Bank, with the original bank vault intact, seems the perfect setting for this extraordinary quilting store. The Old Craft Store, 1110 W. Main St. in Carrollton, has been in business in this location since 1971, supplying quilters with a huge assortment of 100 percent cotton fabrics, wool, books, notions and patterns, as well as inspiring kits and lots of samples. "Hookers" will love the incredible selection of rug hooking supplies. The Old Craft Store is just plain fun! Hours are Monday - Saturday 10 am - 5 pm and until 7 pm on Thursday. Visit www.theoldcraftstorequilting.com or call 972-242-9111.

No matter what style, color, or size quilt you desire to complete your home decorating, you'll find it here at Pierson's Fine Quilts, 1020 W. Main St. This Carrollton treasure houses one of the largest and most beautiful quilt collections in the area. Each quilt is made of 100 per cent cotton and each one passes the "cuddle test!" We also loved the quilted tote bags. The store is open Tuesday - Saturday 10 am - 5 pm. Call 972-242-1507 or visit www.newquilts.com online.

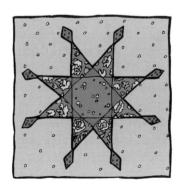

Using old family recipes passed down through generations of wonderful West Texas grandmothers, Mary Beth and Paul Vinyard have created a "fried chicken empire" that sprawls across the Lone Star State. Their first restaurant, "Bubba's Cooks Country" opened in Dallas back in 1981, and was such a success that Babe's Chicken Dinner House soon followed. This location, 1006 W. Main St. in Carrollton, is "Babe's #4" for the Vinyard family, but after one visit, will be your "#1" place to find great fried chicken.

Not only do the recipes date back many years, so does the building! Babe's is located in the old Lyon-Gray Lumber Co.—with the oldest part dating back to the 1930s. A covered patio built of cedar from the Texas Hill Country connects the buildings. And, the old lumber bin has been converted to a private dining room appropriately named "The Chicken Coop."

Nothing says success like the crowds of happy customers who rave about the excellent down-home country cooking at Babe's. Your choices are simple: fried chicken, chicken fried steak, fried chicken fingers, fried catfish, pot roast or hickory smoked chicken, and steaming sides like fluffy buttery mashed potatoes with rich creamy gravy, Grandma's corn, green beans and homemade biscuits that melt in your mouth. Mary Beth says, "The only thing that we make ahead of time is the gravy, because that only gets better as it sits. Everything else we do over and over in tiny batches." According to Paul, the goal for each restaurant is "to make each customer feel like you are eating in your grandmother's kitchen." We think it's better, because you don't even have to help with the dishes!

As the Vinyards continue to garner applause from customers

for their chicken, they have also caught the attention of the Food Network, which featured them in a segment on "Classic Chicken." Plus, *Southern Living Magazine* has touted Babe's Chicken Dinner House as one of their favorites! The atmosphere is casual, the food absolutely delicious and the Vinyard family "like family!" And don't forget to stop by their other fine restaurant: Bubba's Cooks Country. The restaurant is open weekdays 11 am - 2 pm for lunch and 5 - 9 pm for dinner and weekends 11am - 9 pm. For more information, call 972-245-7773. (See page 59 & 232)

(Color photo featured in front section of book.)

Salons, Spas & Indulgence

Treat yourself to a relaxing massage in your own tranquil paradise—Blue Hawaii, Moroccan Cabaret, Solaroma, Cleo's Chambers, The Orient or Jungle Paradise. You can be pampered with a choice of massage treatments available in 30, 45, 60 or 90-minute sessions.

To reduce your stress and promote wellness, owners Beverly and Marcus Hurst, a mother/son team, offer a wide variety of massage services performed by a highly-trained staff, licensed and registered with the State of Texas. Located at 2810 E. Trinity Mills Rd. #127 in Carrollton, hours are Monday-Friday 10 am-8 pm, Saturday 9 am-6 pm and Sunday by appointment. For more information, call 972-418-0081 or visit www.wekneadbodies.com online.

Discover
Cedar Hill/DeSoto
Duncanville/Lancaster

Where does the "Best of the West" begin? The cities of Cedar Hill, DeSoto, Duncanville and Lancaster, Texas, have been designated as "Best Southwest Cities," and enjoy the perfect blend of family, community and business opportunity. They are located in Southwest Dallas County, with breathtaking hillsides, lush natural landscapes and the beautiful Joe Pool Lake. These four cities offer visitors an experience of "small town Texas" with all of the amenities of the big city life that Dallas and Fort Worth have to offer. They are progressive communities with a small-town feel, which is why so many people have settled in this area. But, if you're not lucky enough to call the "Best Southwest Cities" home, we know you'll enjoy visiting them. Cedar Hill, DeSoto, Duncanville and Lancaster share rich historical heritages and proud pasts that point to bright futures. "Best" doesn't even begin to describe these sensational cities!

CEDAR HILL

Cedar Hill is known as the community, "where visitors are treated like neighbors, neighbors are treated like friends, and friends are treated like family!" It is a small, beautiful neighborhood in the "Hill Country of North Texas"—the benefits of the Dallas/Fort Worth Metroplex, without the traffic congestion or industrial sites. Cedar Hill overlooks the 8,500-acre Joe Pool Lake, and boasts the second most visited state park in Texas. Whether you are visiting for a day or decide to stay for a lifetime, you will love the wonderful atmosphere of neighborly smiles and the beautiful community spirit of Cedar Hill.

In the Beginning

Cedar Hill can trace its history to 1847 when one of the first wagon trains brought Mr. Milton Merrifield and his five married sons and their families to the area. They purchased land from Belt Line Rd. to the Trinity River, and soon settlers were following their lead to this beautiful land full of emerald green cedar trees and rolling hills. It is located on part of the "White Rock Escarpment" near the Old Chisholm Trail, and was named Cedar Hill because of the nearby cedar breaks in the Mountain Creek area. After working hard to develop their new hilltop community, the first settlers suffered a huge setback when a tornado swept away almost all of their buildings and claimed at least nine lives. The railroad again came to the defense of this struggling area, making it a commercial center for surrounding farmers and cattlemen. Passenger trains stopped daily in Cedar Hill on their way to major Texas cities like Houston and Dallas.

Here's an interesting historical tidbit. During the 1930s, Raymond Hamilton, a member of the Bonnie and Clyde Gang, robbed the town's bank twice in one week! Legend says that he found out that the manager had dropped some of the cash in the wastebasket, and came back to get it.

A Day Out on the Town

Cedar Hill proudly participates in the Texas Main Street Program, offered by the Texas Historical Commission—constantly working to revitalize the historic downtown district. Today's Cedar Hill Main Street reflects the charm of its past, with architecture that dates to the turn of the century. Visitors love shopping the great downtown boutiques and shops, and can't seem to get enough of that small-town atmosphere so close to the "big city." During the last decade, Cedar Hill has almost exploded with a diverse selection of great dining opportunities including American, Mexican, Oriental, Italian, seafood and more. The town has also become a shopping destination for southern Dallas County, and a popular place for leisure recreation. The 8,500-acre Joe Pool Lake provides great fishing, sailing, boating and water sports. And, Cedar Hill State Park offers day and overnight campers 355 campsites, 30 primitive campsites, a swimming beach, boat ramps, a marina and a restaurant.

Celebrate Cedar Hill!

Visit Cedar Hill during October and you will be treated to a great "Country Day on the Hill." The second Saturday in October is filled with family-oriented activities such as arts and crafts, a 5K run, a dog show, belt sander races, lots and lots of food, and the Lion's Club Fish Fry and Street Dance. Stay till the evening and you can join the traditional Old Settler's Reunion for bingo, beans and cornbread, music, and the big finale—the crowning of King and Queen of the Hill!

December brings the holidays and they are celebrated with lots of fanfare in Cedar Hill. The Old Town Holiday on the Hill is held the first Thursday in December on the historic downtown square. You will enjoy great holiday shopping, as well as music, dancing, games, train rides and, of course, a visit from Santa.

Spring means Fiesta time in Cedar Hill! Fiesta Hispaña celebrates the Hispanic culture in a citywide festival that embraces the culture of south Dallas. The first Saturday of May brings horse shows, live bands, mariachis, low-rider car shows and delicious, spicy food to the Longhorn Stadium, where more than 6,000 visitors learn the meaning of "Fiesta!"

There are many festivals and celebrations throughout the year in Cedar Hill, but "Music in the Park" is by far the favorite. Bring your blanket to the Valley Ridge Park outdoor amphitheater, relax under the stars and enjoy the wonderful live music.

Although you may be just visiting Cedar Hill for a short time, you're sure to feel right at home. In fact, you may never want to leave…

DESOTO

This might be one of those secret little Texas communities virtually unknown to most of you, but DeSoto is one of the up-and-coming places for businesses to grow and prosper. In fact, during its recent "Parade of Homes," many visitors were surprised to find such a booming community, and impressed with the upscale homes and amenities. The setting is one of a beautiful rural countryside filled with friendly, charming people.

Historic DeSoto

One of the oldest settlements in North Texas, DeSoto dates back to 1847, just 11 years after Texas won its independence from Mexico. One of the first pioneers to settle this area was Curtis Parks, who traveled here from Indiana. Other first DeSoto families included Thomas Chesier, Zebedee Heath, Otway B. Nance, Allen Q. Nance, F.N. Hamilton and John P. Voorhies. In 1848, Mr. T. J. Johnson found his way to DeSoto from Tennessee and proceeded to build the first little general merchandise store near what was then called "The Crossroads." The Crossroads was a place where wagon trails intersected; one from Dallas to the Shiloh community in Ellis County, and another east/west trail from Lancaster to Cedar Hill. This "crossroads" is today known as Belt Line and Hampton. A post office was established in 1881, and the town was named to honor Dr. Thomas Hernando DeSoto Stewart, a beloved doctor who was dedicated to the health of the early community.

After World War II, the small town began to flourish, and in 1949, the city of DeSoto became the 19th organized municipality in Dallas County. It was determined at this time that DeSoto had a population of approximately 400 citizens. The city celebrated its 50th anniversary on March 3, 1999.

In 1976, the Texas State Historical Commission awarded a historical marker to one of DeSoto's finest treasures. The Historic Nance Farm is the oldest and finest preserved Antebellum Southern Upland Plantation Farm complex in North Texas. Mr. Otway Bird Nance (1805-1874) traveled all the way from Illinois with his wife and six children to settle in the DeSoto area. He initially purchased 620 acres, and acquired quite a bit of wealth and property during his life. He raised sheep, cattle and horses, and had several domestic and farm-working slaves until the very end of the Civil War. These slaves were probably the workforce behind the building of his farm complex, which included the main house, several small buildings, an 1850s barn and curing shed, an 1880s carriage barn and an early limestone well. There was also a windmill and elevated water tower on the property. An old strong box was found hidden in the attic of the main house, containing exciting historical information. It held quite a few very rare documents dating from the 1850s and 60s concerning land and slaves.

Community Fun

This tranquil, quiet community is close to the Dallas/Fort Worth area, yet remains tucked away amid shady trees, rolling hills, winding creeks and wooded green belts. It is, as they say, "A great place to come home to!" Community involvement is the norm here, where planning for the future is a big priority. Although the city is growing at a fast rate, it maintains its sense of community with special events and festivals. The Fabulous Fourth Fireworks Celebration follows Concerts on the Creek on the Fourth of July, and the Easter Bunny visits DeSoto every spring for the Annual Easter Extravaganza. Toad Holler Creekfest kicks off the summer in DeSoto with arts, crafts, and great entertainment. Bring a picnic dinner and a lawn chair to the free Concerts on the Creek in the outdoor amphitheater. There are numerous great restaurants to try, from mom and pop diners to well-known eateries and private clubs. You'll also enjoy a variety of great shopping opportunities. You will enjoy all that DeSoto has to offer!

DUNCANVILLE

Crawford Trees was among the first settlers to arrive in the area known today as Duncanville. He migrated to Texas from Illinois in 1845, and purchased several thousand acres south of Camp Dallas. In 1855, Mr. Trees donated part of the land so that the area's first school could be built—the Little Bethel Male and Female School.

As with many small Texas towns in this area, Duncanville traces its history to the railroad. It had been a very small settlement until the Chicago, Texas and Mexican Central railroads reached the area in 1880. It was used as a "switching station," and was called "Duncan Switch" in honor of a line foreman. Mr. Charles P. Nance, the community's postmaster, renamed the settlement Duncanville in 1882, and soon telegraph poles and lines were erected in the new town. Although a fire destroyed most of Duncanville's early commercial buildings in 1884, by the turn of the century, there were several dry goods stores, a pharmacy, a new school, two churches, a livery stable, two cotton gins and, of course, a domino parlor! Even though Duncanville had lots to offer, it wasn't exactly a thriving metropolis in the early part of the 1900s. In fact, its population only grew from 113 to 300 folks from 1903 to 1933; however, by 1962 the town had 5,000 residents. It was at that time that the residents adopted a home-rule charter, and the area developed as a thriving Dallas suburb.

Although Duncanville was not incorporated as an official city until 1947, it didn't let that minor detail stop its steady growth. Over the years, it has achieved the prestigious name of, "The City of Champions." We couldn't agree more! Nestled in the rolling wooded hills of southwest Dallas County in some of North Texas' most beautiful scenery, Duncanville is a community of family, good neighbors, and close friends. We're sure it will become one of your favorite places to visit on your day out in the Dallas area.

The City of Champions

Duncanville citizens take pride in the peaceful, friendly atmosphere of their community. They enjoy all of the comforts of a small-town environment with all of the wonderful big-city advantages. They call their city "The City of Champions" for its winning traditions. From the top-notch schools and community services to the strong hometown spirit, Duncanville has "championed" its neighborly atmosphere with amenities that will delight its citizens and visitors. You'll discover a variety of family-owned restaurants, tearooms, and specialty boutiques, giving this town a tranquil, old-fashioned appeal. But, with its close proximity to Dallas and Fort Worth, Duncanville is just minutes from many major attractions. From theater and museums, to parades and festivals, Duncanville is rich in culture and entertainment venues.

Celebrations

This championship city celebrates its heritage and future with great festivals. The Fourth of July Parade and Fireworks Extravaganza is a day filled with activities such as: a parade, fun, food, music, and, of course, spectacular fireworks. The Christmas Parade and Community Tree Lighting is held the first Friday in December, and includes a festive display of holiday spirit, a parade, and the annual lighting of the town's Christmas tree. And, everyone will love the weekly summer concerts on Thursdays. Local parks attract area sports enthusiasts, and golfers will find leading and "championship" golf courses nearby. The Dr Pepper StarCenter double rink ice complex is a major Duncanville attraction, offering a variety of skate programs for all ages. It is the only ice rink in southwest Dallas County—a 95,000 square foot facility with two regulation ice rinks for both beginning and advanced hockey leagues. In fact, it has served as the official practice site of the 2003 State Farm Figure Skating Championships.

City Champions

Duncanville boasts of many wonderful tourist attractions and community success stories, but the real "champions" are her people. The minute you walk into a store, tearoom, or bakery, you will be met with smiling faces and outstretched hands. It is truly a community that cares. You'll find unique shopping and dining experiences for every taste, from a sandwich with an old-time TV theme to elegant cuisine in a ritzy atmosphere. Businesses include flower shops, clothing boutiques, furniture galleries, book and jewelry stores, art galleries, garden shops, and beauty spas. We've found some of the best places in town to help you enjoy Duncanville's "championship shopping experience." So, go for the gold!

LANCASTER

The community of Lancaster is one that celebrates the rural character of the city with the strength and pride of generations gone by. In fact, its rich history and past generations have strengthened the spirit of Lancaster, enabling it to become known as "an historic jewel" of Dallas County. From its very beginning, the residents have reflected an ethnic diversity that has impacted the city with pride and confidence in their future.

It was the first settlement in south Dallas County. Thirty settlers arrived from Green County, Illinois in 1845, settling along the high space on the prairie near Ten Mile Creek. They put up temporary log homes for shelter and tried to scratch out their existence in a land they named "Hardscrabble" (hard: bitter, severe, or harsh and scrabble: to struggle). The name must have reflected the time they had trying to settle the land. Fortunately, the name didn't stick.

Among the first group of settlers in December 1844, was a man named Elder Roderick Rawlins. When the family of Mr. A. Bledsoe moved into the settlement, his daughter married the youngest son of Elder Rawlins in 1852, and this marriage was in essence, the beginnings of Lancaster. Mr. Bledsoe purchased land from the Widow Rawlins and staked out the original town in the same pattern of his birthplace, Lancaster, Ky. Lancaster's historic square is unique because Mr. Bledsoe mapped the streets to enter the square from the center of each side, creating a circular gathering place in the heart of the town. (Much like Independence Square in Philadelphia.) Lancaster's historic square is the only square in Texas that has an English-style architecture.

Lancaster, at this time, was founded as a trading post, and people from all across the area came to trade their wares and shop from the large available stock. Hispanic merchants came to town by way of the Texas Central Highway, which ran from Mexico east to Clarksville. But the Hispanics weren't the only ethnic group. African-American citizens are heavily featured in the stories of early Lancaster.

Devastating Tornado Brings Town Together

On April 25, 1994 a tornado struck the city, doing extensive damage to the downtown and residential areas. A large section of Lancaster's Historic Town Square was also damaged or destroyed. Friends, neighbors and citizens joined forces to clean up and restore the buildings that could be salvaged. Although no longer the shape of a square, visitors continue coming to enjoy food, fun, fellowship and shopping. It will take more than a twister to slow this square down!

The City of Trees

One of the best ways to enjoy this city's rich heritage is to take a walking or driving tour. The town is beautiful, blessed with picturesque surroundings and abundant creeks and woods. In fact, it is known as the "City of Trees." The walking tour will guide you through the Historic Town Square, with its covered sidewalks, sweet shops, restaurants, and gardens that capture the essence of its history. It will also take you through the beautiful Rose Garden at the historic MKT Depot. The rose garden was started with roses from England and you won't want to miss the beautiful white English rose, appropriately named "Lancaster Rose." A short drive will take you to the historic Rawlins House, which was built in 1855. And, you'll want to visit the Strain Farmstead, Lancaster's oldest working farm.

For such a small town, Lancaster has "big city assets," giving it the best opportunities a rural community can afford its citizens and visitors. Within the city are eight shopping centers; a 47-acre greenbelt equipped with hiking trails, playgrounds, and sports activities; an 18-hole Championship Golf Course; and a new community park that includes a state-of-the-art library and amphitheater. The new Lancaster Community Park also offers bike and jogging trails, a pond and fishing pier, picnic shelters with grills, and lighted sports fields. Something for every member of the family! You might want to visit Lancaster on the second Saturdays of the month (excluding January), because there is always a celebration "On the Square." Bring the family for great food, music and entertainment, and enjoy the arts and crafts fair, the flower shows, the chili cookoffs and much more.

Of course, ladies, you are here to discover the great shopping experiences of Lancaster, and you won't be disappointed. The square merchants include precious tearooms, antique shops, gifts, restaurants and yummy bakeries. In fact, the aroma from the downtown bakery warms the entire square, and certainly tempts the taste buds.

For more information about Cedar Hill, contact the Cedar Hill Chamber of Commerce at 972-291-7817, or visit www.cedarhillchamber.org online.

For more information about DeSoto, contact the DeSoto Chamber of Commerce at 972-224-3565, or visit www.desotochamber.org online.

For additional information about Duncanville, contact the Duncanville Chamber of Commerce at 972-780-4990 or visit www.duncanville.com or www.duncanvillechamber.org online.

For more information about Lancaster, contact the Lancaster Chamber of Commerce at 972-227-2579, or visit www.lancasterTX.org online.

Cedar Hill
Fairs Festivals & Fun

May
Fiesta Hispaña
Taste of Cedar Hill & Business Expo

June
Juneteenth Celebration
Music in the Park

October
Annual Golf Tournament
Old Settler's Reunion
Country Day on the Hill Country Fair

December
Old Town Holiday on the Hill

DeSoto Fairs Festivals & Fun

February
Daddy/Daughter Dance

April
Easter Eggstravaganza
Taste of DeSoto

May
Golf Classic
Young Anglers Fishing Tournament – Briarwood Park

June
Best Southwest Juneteenth Celebration
Toad Holler Creek Fest

July
DeSoto's Old Fashioned 4th of July

October
Viva DeSoto - Celebration of Hispanic Heritage

December
Hometown Holiday and Parade of Lights

Duncanville Fairs Festivals & Fun

March
  Business Expo/Art Fest
  Easter Egg Eggstravaganza

April
  ESA Walk/Run

May
  Golf Classic

June
  Summer Music Fest

July
  Stars, Stripes and Sports July 4th Fireworks Celebration
  Summer Music Fest

October
  Annual Auction
  Boo Bash

December
  Christmas Parade and Tree Lighting Ceremony

Lancaster Fairs Festivals & Fun

January
Martin Luther King, Jr. Parade

February
Daddy-Daughter Valentine's Dance
Second Saturday on the Square (February-December)
Chili/Soup/Stew Cook Off

March
Easter Egg Hunt

April
Music Fest Concert (April-June)

May
Cinco de Mayo Celebration
Splash Day at the City Pool

June
Juneteenth Celebration

July
4th of July Celebration and Fireworks Display

August
City of Lancaster Garage Sale
Lions Club Carnival

October
Taste of Lancaster

December
Lions Club Christmas Parade
Tree Lighting Ceremony

LANCASTER TOWN SQUARE

With a list of notable visitors and residents that include the notorious bank robbers Bonnie and Clyde, Sheriff Pat Garrett, outlaw Cole Younger and baseball player Dizzy Dean, Lancaster offers guests a nostalgic look back at the real Old West. Lancaster's Historic Town Square, which was built in 1852, provides a shopping experience in a rustic, real Old West setting. You will find everything from Texas gifts and art to floral arrangements and fun fashion jewelry.

Lit'l Bit Of Texas, 972-227-7955, features a selection of Texas gift baskets, iron yard art and unusual gifts.

Luanna's Women's Clothing Store & Boutique, 972-218-9114, carries the very best in fun fashions for the discriminating shopper.

Backroom Raggs, 972-227-4600, is an "upscale resale" featuring a variety of women's apparel and accessories.

Handscrabble Antiques, 972-218-5829, features Victorian to Art Deco furniture, collectibles, crystal and much more!

And, the **Miz Raus Gift Shop**, 972-227-7287, has Lampe Bergers, Ty Beanie Babies, Yankee, Tyler and Root candles, wind chimes, as well as fun toys.

If there is such a thing as "too much shopping," and you need sustenance for a second wind, take time to enjoy a wonderful meal at one of these great eateries.

The **Cameo Rose Tea Room**, 972-218-7737, will serve you

the finest Tea Room cuisine with homemade entrees and unique desserts.

The Lovin' Oven, 972-227-4425, draws visitors from across the square with the tantalizing aroma of freshly baked breads, pastries, cookies, pies and cakes.

And, **Lettuce Eat Sandwich Shoppe**, 972-227-7039, has sandwiches, soups, salads and made-from-scratch cakes that will keep you coming back for more.

A visit to Lancaster's Old Town Square, 108 N. Dallas Ave., is a memorable event any time of the year, but second Saturdays (February–December) are the best. The Second Saturday Sale offers free entertainment, great shopping and, of course, great food. For information on special events or a complete listing of these and other great Town Square shopping locations, visit online at www.lancastersquare.com or call 972-227-7010.

Knick Knacks
CRAFTS & ANTIQUES MALL

With an entrepreneurial spirit and the support of her husband, Kathy Jones opened her own Duncanville antique mall in 1992, and the experience has been life changing. After having a booth in an antique mall for years, she knew a radical floor design of booth space would aid in customer flow. Knick Knacks Crafts & Antiques Mall is almost 20,000 square feet of shopping and is located at 215 W. Camp Wisdom Rd. All the vendors are extremely friendly, very knowledgeable and the antiques are outstanding. The inventory changes daily, so there is always a reason to go back again and again. And, if you need nourishment from all the shopping—don't worry— a tearoom is only steps away. Don't miss the other location in Arlington at 2801 Division St. Hours are Monday-Saturday 10 am - 6 pm, Thursday until 8 pm and Sunday noon - 5 pm. For more information, visit www.knickknacks.com online or call 972-283-9007.

Artists, Art Galleries, Gifts & Home Décor

After several years of participating in regional craft shows, Bill and Vicki Watkins were encouraged to open a store of their own by their many loyal customers. Having accumulated quite a faithful following for their unique designs of hand-made jewelry and beaded items, they wanted a special place to showcase their pieces. Southwest Corner Gallery, 515 Cedar St. fit the bill. Located in one of Cedar Hill's oldest and most historic buildings, it's the perfect showcase spot. Originally built as the "corner stone" of the early farming community, the building first served as a bank. In fact, it was a very famous bank because it was robbed twice by Raymond Hamilton, part of the notorious Bonnie and Clyde gang!

Today, the windows are filled with beautiful displays of pottery, unique collectibles and hand-made gifts. A visit to the website www.southwestcornergallery.com will reveal a wonderful selection of fine art, hand-made dolls, unique home décor, and, of course, extraordinary, custom-designed jewelry by Bill and Vicki. The Watkins' designs are fashioned with exquisite stones and beautiful craftsmanship, and can be custom made upon request. You will also see religious jewelry by Jeep Collins and wonderful bell pendants by "Jewelry by John."

You will also love the wonderfully unique items for your home, such as handmade soaps in every design imaginable, beautiful crystal and the amazing Lampe Berger fragrance lamps from France that clean the air while scenting the whole room and all with no flame! There is a section for "Everything Texas," decorative crosses and collectibles by All God's Children, Willowtree Angels, Ebony Visions and Daddy's Long Legs.

Southwest Corner Gallery is a delightful mix of beautiful home décor and very special gifts from some of the world's best artists and artisans. Stop by Tuesday - Friday 11 am - 6 pm and Saturday 10 am- 5 pm—open Sundays noon - 4 pm in December. Call 972-293-2123 or 888-4GIFT-4U to learn more.

Glenda Kay Tankersley credits both her earthly and her Heavenly Father with the fulfillment of her 20-year dream. She had watched this historic 1940s Duncanville home at 226 W. Daniel for more than three years in hopes of purchasing it for a gift shop. Suddenly, her dad announced that he was going to buy it, and the wheels were in motion. The home was completely renovated to include an inviting wrap-around porch, which is filled with unique and collectible treasures. Inside, the aroma of a seasonal Tyler Candle fills the air, and the rooms are decorated top to bottom with wonderful gifts. Glenda Kay loves to find unique items such as handmade baby quilts, blankets and towels. We loved the hand-stitched, framed sayings by Kammie's Stitchin' and the hand-painted windows, as well as the very large selection of unique crosses. The store is open Tuesday - Saturday 10 am - 6 pm with extended hours during the holidays. For more information, call 972-296-9898.

Cottage Keepsakes, INC.

Julianne Griffin says that she has been "building and creating" things since she was a little girl. In fact, she won the grand prize in a seventh grade art contest for her entry—a two-story, A-frame dollhouse built perfectly to scale. "Everything was very detailed," she said, "down to the tiny bar of soap I carved from a large bar." She has been taking art classes since sixth grade, and has been involved in community craft shows for many years. So, it's no surprise to her family and friends that she has been successful with her precious store, Cottage Keepsakes, 500 N. Hampton Rd.

The store is located in what visitors remember as Desoto's "Old Nunneley Clinic." They are amazed at the transformation from this clinical atmosphere to a street of quaint shops. Julianne has developed each room with a different theme: Victorian, country, toy warehouse and backyard garden. You will find wonderful antiques, quilts, music boxes and collectibles, as well as frames, soaps, stationery, books, cookie jars, mosaic creations, stained glass and floral arrangements. Don't miss the "Corner Collectibles" room with Boyds Bears and Precious Moments. And, if you're looking for value, check out "Secondhand Roses" where you will find recycled and gently used items. Proceeds from this room benefit the local children's home. Pet lovers will find more than 200 breeds of dog and cat items. Teachers, show your ID for a special 10 percent discount throughout the entire store! Plus, everyone receives the discount on "Build Your Own Gift Baskets."

Julianne enjoys people, so you will usually find her visiting with her customers under the Texas-sized windmills. Be sure to check out her craft workshops for pre-schoolers to grandparents. She teaches everything from clay art to candle making. Cottage Keepsakes' atmosphere is perfect for a morning coffee club, or even a cross-stitch group. The store is open Tuesday-Saturday 10 am-6 pm. Contact Julianne at 972-274-5337.

LANCASTER SECOND SATURDAYS
ON THE SQUARE

Every second Saturday, Lancaster serves up incredible homemade goodies, fantastic bargains, and toe tappin' tunes that keep visitors coming back again and again February–December. Parking and admission are free to Second Saturday, but you'd probably come even if they weren't. You simply have to experience this long-honored tradition. Shop from the many vendors along the covered walkway that surrounds the Square, or enjoy something tasty from every food booth along the way. There is always great entertainment, and lots of friendly Texans that will make you feel right at home in this historic Western town. Also, be aware of the special events and themes featured many Second Saturdays, like October's "Taste of Lancaster," or events like the "Texas Chili Cook Off," the City Wide Garage Sale, Lancaster in Bloom & Pet Parade and Antiques on the Square. To learn more about Lancaster's Second Saturdays Sale, visit www.lancastersquare.com/sale.htm online or call 972-227-7010.

Children's

Baby Delights etc

Baby Delights etc, 610 Cedar St. in Cedar Hill, truly is "delightful." Mother/daughter owners Miriam Frizzell and Naomi Simpson carry Eddie Bauer for boys and Baby Lulu for girls, a large selection of hair bows, and even tiny UT, A&M and OU merchandise. We are not surprised that Baby Delights was voted by *Today Newspapers'* readers "Best of the Best Children's Clothing Store." Open Tuesday - Friday 10 am - 5:30 pm and Saturday until 4 pm. Call 972-291-7844.

Fashion & Accessories

LUANNA'S

Seeking hidden treasure? Tucked away in southwest Dallas County at Luanna's, you will find just that. In business since 1987, this unique boutique features F.L. Malik/Ivy Jane, French Dressing, Picadilly and other fashion-forward lines

and accessories for all ages and sizes. The jewelry alone is worth the trip. Lots of one-of-a-kinds, so come often as inventory changes weekly. Visit at 137 Town Square in Lancaster 10:30 am - 5:30 pm Tuesday - Saturday. Call 972-218-9114 for more information.

When Bill and Vicki Watkins first started selling their jewelry designs at craft shows, they never dreamed that this hobby-turned-business would take over their kitchen table! With the opening of Paradise Cowboy at The Ranch in Cedar Hill, Bill has a work place for his beautiful jewelry designs and Vicki finally gets the family kitchen table back! See this great artist at work, while you shop for fine Southwest collectibles, western décor for the home and the popular Tommy Bahama men's clothing line. Paradise Cowboy, 1427 N. Hwy 67, #200 (Wintergreen Rd. exit), is open Monday - Wednesday 10 am-7 pm, Thursday - Saturday until 8 pm and Sunday noon - 4 pm. For more information, visit www.theparadisecowboy.com or call 972-293-1483.

MERLE NORMAN®

COSMETICS & BOUTIQUE

Sheron Ward visited this Duncanville Merle Norman Cosmetics & Boutique in August 1993, and she loved it so much that she bought it! More than a place to buy makeup, this store offers shoppers an exciting selection of upscale clothing, beautiful jewelry, wonderful accessories and resort clothes. In fact, the resort clothes are so fun and festive, you'll want to plan a cruise. You'll also find unique items that will make any occasion special. Sheron customizes jewelry to match the clothes, and accessorizes the outfits with scarves, flower pins and beautiful day and evening bags.

If you have never had a "Merle Norman makeover," you are in for a treat. The makeup is a wonderful line that matches your individual skin type. Plus, you can see it on before you buy. Merle Norman, 4041 W. Wheatland, #118 (at Hwy. 67), is open Monday-Friday 10 am - 6 pm and Saturday until 4 pm. Call 972-296-2122.

Florists

Jessica's Flowers & Gifts

Let the word slip that your next event is being catered by Jessica's Flowers & Gifts and you won't have an empty seat in the house! Jessica's reputation for scrumptious food and beautiful flowers makes her one of the most sought after caterers and full-service florists in Cedar Hill. Originally from Malaysia where she owned a similar business, Jessica is dedicated to making each event that she caters something to be remembered. Her talent as a creative and energetic floral designer and chef shine through everything she does. All of the items on her catering menu are homemade and delicious—especially her decadent chocolate and divine wedding cakes. Look for a tearoom to open soon within the store. You can also shop for fun gifts such as stuffed animals, Rinconada collectibles and popular "Red Hats!" Jessica's Flowers & Gifts is located at 115 S. Broad St., and is open Monday-Friday 8 am - 6 pm and Saturday until 4 pm. Call 972-291-3848.

Not far from historic downtown Cedar Hill, at 213 N. Hwy. 67 #500A, you will discover a wonderful little slice of "heaven," complete with a casual, friendly atmosphere, an old-fashioned Juke Box, antiques from the 40s and 50s and the heavenly aroma of fresh baked goodies. Must Be Heaven? Yes—It's That Good! Breakfast, lunch and dinner are served daily, along with scrumptious homemade pies and cakes, fresh cookies, hand-dipped ice cream, and other delicious treats. The Heavenly Special is their signature menu item, featuring your choice of select entrees and side dishes. Must Be Heaven prepares quick breakfast items, as well as more than 20 different sandwiches on fresh-baked bread, crisp vegetable and fruit salads, fabulous quiche and soups-of-the-day. Don't forget the "heavenly" desserts (so good they might even be sinful)! The restaurant offers dine-in, take-out, catering and a private dining room. Open Monday - Friday 9 am - 8 pm and Saturday 9 am - 4 pm. For more information, call 972-293-3121 or visit www.mustbeheaven.com online.

Brenham* – 107 W. Alamo, 979-830-8536
Bryan* – 1136 E. Villa Maria, 979-731-8891
College Station* – 1700 Rock Prairie, 979-764-9222
Humble – 9759 FM 1960 Bypass West, 281-446-3232
* A Franchise of Must Be Heaven Holdings, LTD

LETTUCE EAT SANDWICH SHOPPE

Lettuce Eat Sandwich Shoppe, 121 Historic Town Square, is one of Lancaster's most charming restaurants. Both the Coca Cola décor and the very reasonable prices will take you back to the 50s. Every delicious dish is made fresh when you order it. Old fashioned cheeseburgers and hamburgers, chili cheese dogs and nachos are always popular, but for lighter fare you may order the grilled chicken salad, tuna plate or delicious soup. End with a slice of homemade cake topped with Blue Bell ice cream! Lettuce Eat is open Tuesday-Saturday 10 am-3pm. Call 972-227-7039.

CAMPUZANO
mexican food

Be sure and check out Campuzano Mexican Food of Cedar Hill at 213 W. Belt Line. See page 256 for full details.

Salons, Spas & Indulgence

Remède Spa & Wellness Center

Remède Spa & Wellness Center can be found at 100 S. Main St., #104 in Duncanville. The spa has a cozy atmosphere and is located in the new, upscale Main Station Building. Remède Spa offers an array of massages, customized facials, body wraps, manicures and pedicures, an aroma steam cabinet, and so much more. Let your mind and body escape in the Rejuvenation Room, a sanctuary dedicated to relaxation, or take advantage of the unique Treatment Suite for Two, designed for couples or girlfriends to share their experience. Allow for extra time to arouse your senses in the boutique full of candles, aromatherapy, lotions and potions. Don't forget to take home a gift of your experience, so you can extend the serenity. Whether you are a guest for an hour or a day, once inside and far away from daily life, you will lose yourself in the tranquility of Remède. The spa is open Monday-Saturday—hours vary. Call 972-572-1772 or visit www.remedespa.net online to embark on a journey you won't soon forget.

Discover
Coppell/Irving

COPPELL

Although the city of Coppell was not officially incorporated until 1955, settlers began finding their way to the area in the 1840s. The area was on the original land grant of Mr. J. A. Simmonds. History tells us that President Sam Houston and the Republic of Texas troops camped on the Grapevine Creek in 1843, while trying to enlist the aid of area Indian tribes against attacks by Mexican soldiers. The first known settler was Mr. James Parish of Goliad. In 1873, the community was known only as "Gibbs" in honor of Barnett Gibbs, a former Texas Senator and Lieutenant Governor. In 1890, the community changed its name to Coppell in honor of Mr. George Coppell, the engineer credited with bringing the railroad to town. It was the Cotton Belt Railroad (part of the St. Louis and Southwestern Texas Railroad) that remained the major form of transportation until the 1920s. That's when paved roads brought automobiles to the area.

History buff? Visit the historical Bethel Cemetery at Christi Lane and Moore Road to see graves of early Texas pioneers, including Revolutionary and Civil War veterans, Indians, and several slaves. You will also see an old-fashioned barbershop in Old Town Coppell that has stood the test of time.

Coppell Community Spirit

The friendly, hometown spirit that embodies the people of Coppell is evident in the many ways they give back to their community. The perfect example is the Coppell Community Garden, which cultivates more than delicious produce. The Community Garden was established in 1998 to "promote social cohesiveness, civic awareness and service, nutritional and food production benefits, environmental stewardship, and great opportunities for education, therapy and recreation." Volunteer gardeners donate time and knowledge in producing more than 27,000 pounds of fresh produce, which gets donated to families in need. The Garden has been an excellent place for youth organizations of Coppell to get involved with Service Learning Projects and Community Service.

Captivating Coppell

Over the years, Coppell has maintained a wonderful blend of big city flare and small-town rural charm—very traditional, yet extremely modern, with a perfect balance of culture and recreation. You might even see horses grazing within the city limits! Present-day Coppell is a thriving city just 20 miles from Dallas, with a population of nearly 38,000. The recreational activities in this small city are endless. Nearby parks and lakes, as well as biking trails and golf courses offer hours of wonderful family entertainment. Coppell also boasts an extraordinary symphony orchestra with performances year round, and a remarkable Community Theatre, which produces and stages five shows per season.

IRVING

From championship golf and professional football to boutiques and bistros, Irving offers something for everyone. Conveniently located between Dallas and Fort Worth, this Texas town is packed full of wonderful activities to satisfy any preference.

A Historic Namesake

Settlers made their way to this area in the 1850s. The new town was founded in 1903 by J. O. Schulze and Otis Brown and incorporated in 1914. The history of the name has two versions and the first version is as follows:

Brown chose to name the city Irving after his wife's favorite author, Washington Irving. Recognized as "America's First Man of Letters," Washington Irving's most recognized works include "The Legend of Sleepy Hollow" and "Rip Van Winkle." The City Council adopted author Washington Irving as the city's namesake in 1998.

The second version appeared in 1953 in *The Dallas Morning News*.

According to the article, dozens of name suggestions were made, but all were rejected. After months of delay, the new post office was named Irving around 1903. More than 50 years later Brown and Shultze still argued good-naturedly about the origin of the town's name. According to Shultze, Brown was corresponding with a young lady in the West named Irvine. Shultze thinks that the name Irving popped into Brown's mind from that.

We will let you decide your favorite version…

In the early part of the 20th Century, Irving became a center for dairy farming, poultry production and cotton farming. By 1920, the population was around 350, and despite the looming depression, Irving continued to grow. The 1950s ushered in many things that guaranteed a promising future for the city, including the University of Dallas and Plymouth Park Shopping Center. Home building exploded to keep up with the population, which had grown to 45,895 by 1960.

The 1970s would prove to be a very busy and exciting time for Irving. In 1971, Irving found itself as the newest home to the Dallas Cowboys football team when Texas Stadium first opened its doors. But one of the most monumental events of the century occurred in 1974 with the opening of DFW International Airport on the northern and western borders of the city. The airport has proven to be a major economic generator, leading to major commercial and residential development for the city. Leading an unparalleled urban development was Ben H. Carpenter with the establishment of the world-renowned Las Colinas development in 1973, which spurred years of significant growth and development in the 1980s.

Hip Hip Hooray for Irving!

Irving has an easy-going spirit and exceptional opportunities for recreation and relaxation. Some of the city's more popular attractions include Texas Stadium, Movie Studios Tour at Las Colinas, the National Scouting Museum and Norman Rockwell Art Gallery, Las Colinas Equestrian Center and Polo Club, and authentic Venetian gondola cruises on the Mandalay Canal, in addition to ballet and theater productions, symphonies and the world's largest equestrian sculpture.

"The Mustangs of Las Colinas," a remarkable bronze sculpture of nine beautiful mustangs galloping across a granite stream, is the work of African wildlife artist Robert Glen. This famous sculpture was installed in 1984 at Williams Square Plaza in the Las Colinas Urban Center as a memorial to the heritage of Texas. Located nearby is the Mustang Sculpture Exhibit, which includes an informative video featuring country music recording artist and North Texas native LeAnn Rimes.

For shopping in Irving, visit the downtown Heritage District, which features antique stores, tearooms, boutiques and even an old-fashioned soda fountain. You will find fabulous shopping and friendly shop owners eager to help you in the Heritage District.

For more information about Coppell, contact the Coppell Chamber of Commerce at 972-393-2829 or visit www.coppellchamber.org online.

For additional information about Irving, contact the Irving Convention and Visitors Bureau at 972-252-7476, 800-2-IRVING or visit online at www.irvingtexas.com. Or, contact the Greater Irving-Las Colinas Chamber of Commerce at 972-252-8484 or visit www.irvingchamber.com online.

Coppell Fairs Festivals & Fun

February
  Dad and Daughter Sweetheart Ball
  Mom and Son Sweetheart Ball

March
  Chamber Annual Gala
  Community Egg Hunt
  Family Fish

April
  Arbor Day Celebration
  Clean Coppell - Earthfest

June
  Farmers Market (June – October)

July
  Spirit of Coppell, July 4th Celebration

August
  Water Conservation Day – Tours of SmartScapes

October
  Halloween Fair and Hayride
  Wildflower Planting

December
  Holiday Parade and Open House

Irving
Fairs Festivals & Fun

March
Dallas Divas
KSCS Country Fair

April
Rockin' 50s Day and Car Show

May
Las Colinas Polo (May-July)
Polo on the Lawn
Big D Charity Horseshow
Cinco de Mayo
EDS Bryon Nelson Championship
Downtown Rhapsody

June
Heritage Festival

July
4th of July Pops Concert & Fireworks
Independence Day Parade and Patriotic Program

August
Dallas Cowboys Football (August-December)

September
Diez y Seis Festival

October
Main Event

December
Holiday Extravaganza Parade and Tree Lighting

IRVING ANTIQUE MALL

Ask anyone in Irving for the best place to find wonderful antiques and you will be directed to the Irving Antique Mall, 129 S. Main St. Here you'll find more than 30 individual dealers, with their treasures displayed in separate charming vignettes. And, behind the main desk, you will always find Jimmie Zinn. Jimmie and husband Tommy Zinn have lived in Irving and been married  more than 43 years and are delightful owners and business people who have earned the respect of their long-time customers.

We found wonderful collections of beautiful Depression glass and coins, cookie jars, and antique china, as well as jewelry, pottery and rare books. As you stroll through the mall and visit with each of the dealers, you'll meet sweet people, who are very knowledgeable about their antiques. The Irving Antique Mall is open Monday-Saturday 10 am - 6 pm. For more information, call 972-254-0339.

Jewelry

CARDONA & CAMPBELL
JEWELERS

Located in Irving's Heritage District at 129 S. Main St. off Irving Blvd., Cardona & Campbell Jewelers offers beautiful estate jewelry, fashion jewelry by local artists, and small gift items. You can take your jewelry there for repair, as well as have your own custom work done. Owners Dora Martinez and Jonna Zambrano named the store for Dora's mother and Jonna's great grandmother, both strong women for their times. Open Monday-Saturday 10 am-6 pm. For more information, call 972-571-9255.

Restaurants

The minute you taste the first chip dipped in the homemade salsa, you'll be hooked! The entire Herrera family makes sure of that. Ole's Tex-Mex, 600 E. Sandy Lake Rd. #106, is a Coppell favorite for some of the most authentic, most delicious Mexican food you will find anywhere. The recipes have been passed down through generations, and the dishes are presented with a festive flair. Their specialties include unique items like Chile Relleno, Shrimp Burrito and Carne Guidsada. We loved the Pechugas—seasoned, grilled chicken breasts topped with a variety of wonderful dressings such as sautéed onion rings, mushrooms, zucchini, sour cream and spicy red sauce. Save room for a true Mexican treat—Fried Ice Cream!

Don't miss the other fine Herrera family restaurants, La Sierra Mexican Grille, located at 2221 Cross Timbers Rd. #105, and El Camaron Pelao Mexican Seafood, 2321 Cross Timbers Rd. #405, in Flower Mound. (See page 127.)

Ole's Tex Mex is open Monday-Thursday 11 am-9 pm, Friday and Saturday until 10 pm and Sunday 9 am-9 pm. For more information, call 972-393-7510.

Be sure and check out Mama's Daughters' Diner in Irving at 2412 W. Shady Grove. See page 172 for full details.

Salons, Spas & Indulgence

SALON
ON THE **Creek**

A Full Service Day Spa

Lyne Norris has been "making people beautiful" all of her life—or at least most of it. She actually started in the "beauty business" at the young age of 14, and was licensed as a stylist at the age of 17! Lyne gained quite a name for herself acting as stylist for many of the contestants in the Miss Texas and Miss America Programs. Her beautiful new salon and day spa, Salon on the Creek, is located in Coppell at 684 S. Denton Tap Rd. #100, and backs up to a beautiful little creek. The view from the patio is very peaceful, and the quiet serenity of the salon provides the perfect atmosphere for a relaxing day at the spa. Lyne has 18 hair stylists; three nail techs; a massage therapist; and a facial specialist. All are experienced professionals who are dedicated to making your visit a special memory. Salon on the Creek is open Tuesday - Thursday 9 am - 8 pm, Friday until 6pm and Saturday 8 am - 4 pm. Call 972-462-1388.

Discover
Flower Mound

In the Beginning

This charming little North Texas town gets its unusual name from a 12.5-acre mound of land that historians date back to the early 1800s. It is believed to have been a sacred ceremonial ground used by the Wichita Indians, and was covered with blue stem grasses and a variety of indigenous flowers. This unusual mound of land is located near the intersection of FM 3040 and FM 2499, and has been declared a historical site. It is as beautiful now as it was then so you won't want to miss it!

By Leaps and Bounds

Today, Flower Mound has a population of more than 59,900, with a future that promises phenomenal growth. In fact, it held the title of the "Second Fastest Growing City in Texas" for much of the 1990s. The town encompasses 44 square miles deep in the heart of the Metroplex, just minutes from Dallas/Fort Worth International Airport, so residents say they are "10 minutes from anywhere in the world!"

Outdoor Fun

Flower Mound is also beautifully situated between two large lakes—Lake Grapevine on the south, and Lake Lewisville to the north. This fortunate location offers visitors access to the heavily wooded hills, and an abundance of creeks and shorelines. It is also home to the Cross Timbers Region, which is one of the largest natural hardwood forests in the entire country. The town's Parks and Recreation facilities include parks with more than 500 acres of playscapes, picnic areas, barbecue grills, walking trails and fun! There are more than 30 miles of nationally recognized trails connecting the parks, neighborhoods, schools and businesses, so you'll see many of the locals "experiencing the great outdoors."

If you have a husband whose mission is to try all of the North Texas Golf Courses, he'll want to play Flower Mound's two nationally-recognized courses, Tour 18 and Bridlewood. You can plan something fun for the entire family, and still have time for great shopping!

For more information about Flower Mound, visit the Flower Mound Chamber of Commerce online at www.flowermoundchamber.com or call 972-539-0500. Or, you may wish to contact the Town of Flower Mound at 972-874-6000 or visit www.flower-mound.com online.

Flower Mound Fairs Festivals & Fun

January
   Rainbow Trout Kidfish

April
   Easter Egg Scramble
   Father/Daughter Prom

May
   Cross Timbers Classic Bike Tour

July
   Celebrate America Family Picnic
   Children's Parade and Fireworks Show

August
   Highland Village Balloon Festival

September
   Fiesta Flower Mound

October
   Halloween Lock-In

November
   Metric Half-Marathon
   Mother/Son Hoe Down
   Veterans Day Remembrance Ceremony

December
   Christmas Parade
   Holiday Stroll

Chapelle des Fleurs

Finally, there's a place to go in the Flower Mound area to celebrate your wedding in style! After 28 years in the party and catering business, Janice Doreen Orndorf has now opened a delightful chapel and reception site in Flower Mound. Each wedding or party is completely personalized to suit your taste, with heavy hors d'oeuvre buffets or elegant sit down dinners. You'll love the extra special touches such as fresh flowers on cakes.

With the need for a non-denominational chapel and reception facility that is not a hotel or country club, this very elegant chapel provides the perfect site for your wedding celebration. The chapel, done in Old World Country French décor, seats more than 200 guests and is available not only for weddings, but also for church services, funerals and corporate functions. Its custom-made pews, leaded windows and 17 chandeliers make it the only one of its kind in the area. With a built-in dance floor and bar area, there is room for 300 guests at your party or reception.

Janice, a lifetime member of the national registry of Who's Who in the U.S.A. in Catering and Floral Design, has worked with more than 2,000 brides. She offers four packages for the bride-to-be and all are "gems." Choose from pearl, diamond, ruby or emerald packages.

Located in Flower Mound at 2701 Corporate Dr. between Hwy. 407 and Main St. off Hwy. 2499, Chapelle des Fleurs is open for functions and consultations by appointment only. Call 214-513-7747 for an appointment or visit www.chapelledesfleurs.com online.

Children's

⟨Once upon a child®

At Once Upon a Child, you'll find an unbelievable selection of "Kids' Stuff with Previous Experience"®—gently used children's clothing, costumes and accessories—newborn to size 10, in excellent condition and at affordable prices. With a large inventory of gently used children's furniture and equipment, owners Rachel Wilson and Julé Miller offer terrific deals on cribs, bouncy chairs and decorative items for the nursery.

There's even a convenient play area for toddlers who would rather watch cartoons and play with toys while you shop. Rachel and Julé also pay up front for your gently used items, when accepted.

Located at 2311 Cross Timbers, #317 in Flower Mound, Once Upon A Child is open Monday-Friday 10 am-7 pm, Saturday 10 am-6 pm and Sunday noon-5 pm. For more information, call 972-874-0779 or go to www.ouac.com online.

Bella Rosa, owned-and-operated by Tammy Foster and her daughters, is located in the "Shops at Flower Mound," 2021 FM 407, #249. You will find clothes, shoes and accessories from casual to dressy to funky to functional—there is something for every woman. Sisters Stacey Foster and Shelley Smith make Stone 'N' String® custom jewelry, incorporating semiprecious stones and sterling silver! Stop by 10 am-7 pm Monday-Friday, 10 am-6 pm Saturday and 1-5 pm Sunday. Call 972-691-5556.

The trendy, label-conscious teen will love shopping here where owners Rachel Wilson and Julé Miller offer a huge selection of gently used, designer clothing and accessories. You'll find jeans, shirts, shoes and jewelry. Located at 2311 Cross Timbers, #305 in Flower Mound, Plato's Closet is open Monday-Friday 10 am-8 pm, Saturday 10 am-6 pm and Sunday noon-5 pm. For more information, visit www.platoscloset.com online or call 972-691-8988.

Furniture, Gifts, Home Décor & Interior Design

No Place Like Home

When Suejo Allen and Freddie Kay Henry decided to open a gift shop, their goal was "to have attractive, quality items at affordable prices for the home decorator." No Place Like Home, 2608 Long Prarie Rd. #204, surpassed even their expectations as it blossomed into one of Flower Mound's most impressive and popular shops. You'll find exquisite tapestries, wall sconces, framed art, unique iron pieces, tabletop décor, throws, clocks and decorative boxes and plates. And, you'll recognize famous names such as Arthur Court and Byers' Choice Carolers. Suejo and Freddie find unique items at market, as well as products from local artisans. They buy often and in small quantities so that their store is constantly changing. Open Monday-Friday 10 am-5:30 pm and Saturday until 4:00. Call 972-899-1937.

CONSIGN & Design

HOME FURNISHINGS

Susan Mittan and her husband prayed earnestly about what type of business would best utilize her talents. The divine result— Consign and Design Home Furnishings, 2311 Cross Timbers Rd. #307 in Flower Mound. The store is a beautifully decorated showroom filled with quality consignment and new furniture, as well as accessories that truly make a house a home. Customers love the fact that Susan will come to their homes for décor consultations and offer design ideas. Susan is a warm, friendly and very creative person who loves helping people. Her business has been so successful—and so much fun—that she has expanded into the space next door. You will love everything about this store, from the inviting fragrance and remarkable furniture to the warm and gracious welcome you'll receive from Susan and her staff. The store is open Monday, Wednesday, Friday and Saturday 10 am-6 pm, and Tuesday and Thursday until 7 pm. Call 972-539-0910.

Gardens & Nurseries

Providing consistent quality service to southern Denton County communities, Woody's Landscape is a company you can trust. Named Business Woman of the Year in Flower Mound, owner Cheryl Smith works with many Chambers of Commerce and civic organizations. Woody's Landscape, 114 Gotcher Ave. in Lake Dallas, is open Monday-Friday. Gift certificates are available. Visit www.woodyslandscape@centurytel.net or call 940-321-4125 or 972-221-9181.

Jewelry & Specialty Shops

Wrap It Up

Carol Anne Crossan is in business to make you look great in two different ways. First, she offers a fabulous selection of freshwater pearl and gemstone jewelry. Consider a custom made design for your bridal jewelry or any special occasion. Second, you'll be the favorite gift-giver in Flower Mound or any town, when your friends receive one of her unique gift baskets. Call 972-691-9623 for an appointment or visit www.pearlwrap.com online to "wrap up" all your gift giving needs.

Restaurants

From the delicious homemade salsa to the last crumb of Sopapilla, you will love everything about this festive, popular Flower Mound restaurant. La Sierra Mexican Grill, 2221 Cross Timbers Rd. #105, is one of three restaurants owned by the respected Herrera family. The atmosphere is very colorful and fun, but the main attraction is the delicious, authentic Mexican food. The recipes have been in their family for generations, tweaked sometimes to keep with the latest trends. For instance, you will find several low-carb meals on the menu, as well as the traditional dishes such as Enchiladas, Fajitas, Chile, Quesadillas and Pechugas. You can also try seafood (with a Mexican twist)! Save just a little room for a wonderful dessert like Mexican Flan, Pralines or Fried Ice Cream!

Don't miss the other fine Herrera family restaurants, Ole's Tex-Mex, located at 600 E. Sandy Lake Rd., in Coppell and El Camaron Pelao Mexican Seafood, 2321 Cross Timbers Rd., #405, in Flower Mound. (See page 116.)

La Sierra Mexican Grill is open Sunday-Thursday 11 am-9 pm and Friday-Saturday until 10 pm. For more information, call 214-513-8718.

Discover Forney

Bordering the East Fork of the Trinity River just 20 minutes east of downtown Dallas, with terrain that varies from scenic rolling wooded hills to flat blackland prairie, Forney is a distinct blend of old and new. It has a small-town relaxed atmosphere, friendly folks, and some of the best antique stores in the state. In fact, in 1987 Forney was named the "Antique Capital of Texas" by the State Legislature.

The Old Forney

Stories about the rolling prairies and good farmland in North Central Texas enticed farmers and ranchers to this area as early as 1847. History claims that Sallie Daugherty and her four sons were the first family to settle the area when she purchased 1,000 acres of land just four miles southeast of present-day Forney. She named it Union Hill, which later became known as Lone Elm. The town was to change names several times until the 1870s when the Texas and Pacific Railroad came through the town and changed its future forever. When the original town name of Brooklyn was submitted so that a post office could be established, there was already another town with the same name. Local citizens chose to rename it Forney, after John W. Forney, the director of the Texas and Pacific Railroad.

The good farmland and rolling prairies that had attracted the first settlers proved to be the town's most important resource. The prairies were covered with a sweet native grass that produced very nutritious hay when cut and baled. This hay was one of Forney's leading exports. By 1910, Forney had eight cotton gins, which yielded fifteen to twenty thousand bales of cotton that were shipped to markets across the country.

The New Forney

Forney continued to thrive until World War II, when, like many small Texas towns, business came to a standstill. It wasn't until the late 1960s that Forney began to take on a new status. Glen "Red" Whaley opened the first antique business in East Forney, which was the impetus for the reputation it has today. Now, there are dozens of antique stores, both wholesale and retail located in and around the city featuring both American and European antiques. It is a town that is considered an ideal place to live, work or visit. Its forward-thinking government, excellent school system (and great football team), beautiful historic homes and excellent recreation and shopping opportunities make Forney the perfect blend of "old and new."

For more information about Forney, contact the Forney Chamber of Commerce online at www.forney-texas.com/chamber or call 972-564-2233. Or, contact the Forney Economic Development Corporation at 972-564-5808.

Forney Fairs Festivals & Fun

May
Forney Chamber of Commerce Civic Auction

July
July 4th Fireworks Display

September
Jackrabbit Stampede

October
Chamber of Commerce Golf Tournament
Fall Festival

December
Forney's Hometown Christmas

Antiques

WHOLESALE ANTIQUES

When Dean Stevenson entered the antique business after retirement, he soon learned that there was an abundance of European and English antiques available, but that American antiques were scarce. Wholesale Antiques, 10524 W. U.S. Hwy. 80 in Forney, is now one of the largest sources of American antiques in the Southwest, catering to the public, designers and the trade-market. Wholesale Antiques specializes particularly in Mahogany, Hepplewhite and Duncan Phyfe style dining room and bedroom furniture dating from the 1920s to the 1950s. Dean and his staff enjoy working with customers and dealers to find furniture that suits special requests, including large dining sets with eight, 10 or 12 chairs. You will also find turn-of-the-century American Oak and Walnut antiques. They ship coast-to-coast and overseas, and have even shipped furniture to the "First Families" of the United States and Mexico! The store is open Tuesday-Saturday 11 am - 5:30 pm and Sunday noon - 5:30 pm. For more information, visit www.deanswholesaleantiques.com online or call 972-564-4433.

MEMORIES GALORE ANTIQUES
& BACK IN THE OLDEN DAYS RESTAURANT

One day, Rhonda DeVilbiss decided she wanted to make a living doing something fun—and we are so glad she did! Because of her love for food, antiques and her experience gained from 25 years in the corporate world, she successfully opened Memories Galore Antiques & Back in the Olden Days Restaurant. You'll find everything from salt spoons and glassware to armoires and sideboards, Shabby Chic and primitives to American and European fine furniture. Then, top your shopping experience off with a delicious lunch at the Back in the Olden Days Restaurant. What a wonderful way to spend the day! Memories Galore is located at 10758 W. U.S. Hwy. 80, Bldg. 9 & 10, in Forney—the "Official Antique Capital of Texas." There are more than 100 dealers, the best prices in town, and a fabulous menu. Open six days a week 10 am-5 pm, closed Wednesdays. For more information, contact Rhonda at 972-564-2188.

D J L Antiques
Custom Frames & Gallery

As part of Forney's famous "antique row," DJL Antiques certainly lives up to its reputation of being one of the most wonderful antique businesses in town. Inside you will find rows and rows of original and rustic antiques and reproductions from all over the world. Owner K. Dieter Esch dreamed of coming to the United States from Germany and opening his own antique store. He has successfully made both of those dreams come true. In fact, he has been in the antique business for more than 20 years and has become an expert framer. DJL Antiques is located at 10500 W. U.S. Hwy. 80 in a large metal warehouse and is open daily 10 am-5 pm. You can't miss it—just look for the large farm carts outside. For more information, contact Dieter at 972-564-6969.

ANTIQUES EAST
A Collection of Shops

Family-owned-and-operated since 1985, Antiques East was one of the first antique malls in the Dallas area. It is located at 10486 W. U.S. Hwy. 80 in Forney. With more than 20,000 square feet in two buildings, more than 80 antique dealers showcase everything from glassware and dinnerware to collectible toys, memorabilia, and furniture. And, if that isn't enough, they have a second location at 10470 W. U.S. Hwy. 80. Antiques East is open Monday-Saturday 10 am - 5 pm and Sunday noon - 5 pm. For more information, call owner Roe England at 972-564-1303.

Whispering Winds

After retiring from Baylor Medical Center, Helen Boykin was able to realize a long-time dream—opening Whispering Winds Antiques & Collectibles. The store is located at 10562 W. U.S. Hwy 80 in Forney's famous antique row, and is an eclectic collection of treasures for discerning customers. Helen has wonderful vintage furniture, beautiful crystal, candles, lamps and the popular Willow Tree Angels. Whispering Winds is open Thursday-Friday 11 am-5:00 pm, Saturday until 5:30 pm, and Sunday noon-5:30 pm. For more information, call 972-564-4474 or visit www.whispernwinds.com online.

Books, Cafés & Coffee

With a servant's heart and a love of people, Shelley Allen opened her business—The Servant's Bookstore and Coffee Bar, 101 E. Grove St. in Kaufman (just 15 miles southeast of Forney). The store is located in what was once the first grocery store in Kaufman County, then the Fuller Uniform Company for more than 60 years. It is now filled with beautiful antiques and stained glass partitions, Thomas Kinkade art, crosses of every material and style, and books, books, books. Shelley admits that she is a "book-a-holic," and a perpetual student, and loves helping Christian families educate their children. She says that her store is a "cross between Starbucks, Family Christian Stores, Borders and Mardel's." Her materials include Christian education materials, history, travel, gardening, art, hobbies, science, music and biographies. The coffee bar features specialty, decadent desserts—homemade right here in Kaufman. The Servant's Bookstore and Coffee Bar is open Monday-Friday 7:30 am - 6 pm and Saturday 8 am - 8 pm. Call 972-962-BOOK or visit www.theservantsbookstore.com online.

THE DAILY GRIND

Customers can't quite explain it, but the rustic, homey atmosphere of this popular Forney coffee shop is mesmerizing. With a piping hot latte and delicious scone, they feel the weight of the world melt away and they never want to leave! The Daily Grind Coffee Bar & Café, 121 E. U.S. Hwy 80, was given a three-star rating by the *Dallas Morning News* in December, 2003. Sisters Julie Bradshaw and Linda Smallwood are famous for their gourmet coffees and teas, as well as their wonderful sandwiches and wraps, low-carb items, cheesecakes and desserts. Try the Guacamole Gobbler Wrap or the Jack Rabbit Special—white chocolate and caramel latte! For more information and hours, call The Daily Grind at 972-564-JAVA.

A woman is like a tea bag...you don't know how strong she is until you put her in hot water.

— *Eleanor Roosevelt*

Amish Furniture Showcase

Heirloom-quality, handmade hardwood furniture says it all when describing the beautiful furniture at Amish Furniture Showcase, located at 125 E. U.S. Hwy. 80 in Forney. Choose from oak, cherry, maple, hickory, walnut and quartersawn oak, and numerous stains to fit your individual décor. Family-owned-and-operated, we also offer Mrs. Miller's jams, jellies, salsa and pasta sauces. Many other gift items are also available: candles, iron crosses, scripture pottery, toys and other wood items for accenting your home. For a sample of their inventory, visit www.amishfurnitureshowcase.com online. Amish Furniture Showcase is open Monday-Saturday 10 am-6 pm. For more information, call 972-564-2772.

Discover Gainesville

Cattle Drives, Circus Clowns and Elephants

With a colorful (and sometimes raucous) past, no one has ever called Gainesville a dull little "cow town." Settled in 1850, the town was a stop on the Butterfield Stage line beginning in 1858.

Throughout the late 1800s, Gainesville became a bustling cattle town because of its location between the Chisholm and Sedalia Trails. Cattlemen from all over North Texas began depositing millions of dollars into the local banks, spurring quite a boom for the town.

Of course along with the millions of dollars and successful cattle drives came the rough and rowdy cowboys and their lifestyle. Gainesville was the last stop for the cowboys before they entered Indian Territory. It represented a last chance to experience "civilization"—buy supplies, clean up by swimming nude in Elm Creek, and then go and gamble and enjoy the nightlife and all it offered at the many saloons on Commerce Street. If you look closely at many of the historic buildings in downtown Gainesville, you can still see faint writings, identifying them as saloons.

If you have a chance to tour the historic Lindsay House on East California St. you will read accounts of the numerous business transactions that took place there during the 1800s. The Lindsay House was the site for two Cattle Raisers Association Conventions during the 1800s. For the ball for the 1888 convention, a local cattleman's wife ordered a ball gown from Paris at a cost of $1500. Cattlemen from all over North Texas and the Panhandle listed their address as Gainesville.

Much of the history of the community can be explored at

the Morton Museum of Cooke County, the local county historical museum, which is located one block south of the National Register Cooke County Courthouse in the 1884 former City Hall-Fire Station-Jail.

With the coming of the railroad to Gainesville in 1879, followed by a second line in 1887, the prosperity of the community increased. Today the Santa Fe Depot is still a working train station where the Amtrak's Heartland Flyer makes two stops a day round trip from Oklahoma City to Fort Worth. You can also tour the Santa Fe Depot Museum to see exhibits that highlight the impact of transportation in Gainesville, as well as a newsreel featuring the Gainesville Community Circus.

One of the most exciting times in Gainesville's history was the opening of the Gainesville Community Circus. The all-volunteer circus was "the only show of its kind in the world" and delighted children and families for more than 28 years. Local citizens performed in the traveling burlesque circus, which was started as a fundraising project for the Gainesville Little Theater. A serious fire in 1954, which destroyed a lot of the equipment and from which the circus never completely recovered, led to the decision to disband the three-ring circus eight years later. Circus performers were instrumental in opening the Frank Buck Zoo where many of the animals were placed with new animals being added over the years. The zoo was named for the famous pioneer of modern era zoos, Gainesville native Frank "Bring 'em Back Alive" Buck. The Frank Buck Zoo has remained an integral part of Gainesville's culture through the years and is one the city's number one attractions.

Medal of Honor

Gainesville is the first city in the nation to establish The Medal of Honor Host City Program. The program's purpose is to recognize legendary, humble heroes who, through great personal sacrifice, have preserved our freedoms. The program pays tribute to the foundations that this medal represents—duty, donor and country. While visiting Gainesville, all Medal of Honor recipients receive funding to cover lodging, food and fuel expenses. Not only does this help the Medal of Honor recipients, it also exposes the citizens of Gainesville to these role models of selfless service. The men of valor are invited to share experiences with students, clubs and local organizations. The city also honors these special visitors with trees planted in the Home Grown Hero Walking Trail.

Follow the Red Brick Streets!

Gainesville is a city that is famous for its classic brick-paved streets and beautiful 19th century brick Victorian homes. Take a walk or drive down Church, Denton and Lindsay Streets to see approximately 26 spectacular historic homes, many of which were designed and built by architect John Garrett. Located on Church Street are two beautiful homes that were built by best friends, English cotton brokers Robert Timmis and Ralph Moodie. The Timmis House, which was built in 1906, remains in its original shingle style today. The Moodie House, which was built in 1910 as a replica of his best friend's house, has been extensively renovated, and now presents an impressive Federal façade. Timmis and Moodie played a role in history, when during World War I they boarded the ship the Lusitania in 1915 and headed for England. On May 7, 1915 a German torpedo sank the ship. The two men gave up their life jackets to a woman and her child who did not have any. Only one of the friends survived the disaster and returned to Gainesville.

If you have time, be sure to take a scenic drive down Farm Roads 678, 372 and 902 to capture the rolling hills of the Cross Timbers region and witness the breathtaking marvels of the untainted landscape.

Discovering all of Gainesville's treasures will send you on an expedition through old and new. The charming historic district is filled with beautiful architecture and history, antique stores, specialty shops and museums that will keep you busy for days. An active Main Street program continues to preserve the integrity of Gainesville's history with a confident eye on its future. Along with your tour of the Victorian homes, be sure to visit the many beautiful churches that also reflect the history of Gainesville. Saint Paul's Episcopal Church on East California St. was built from local brick and limestone hauled by ox-cart from a local quarry. The First United Methodist Church and the First Presbyterian Church are both located on South Denton, and are beautiful examples of historic craftsmanship. Downtown visitors will hear the chime of church bells on the hour, with hymns played on the bells at 10 am, noon and 6 pm.

Till Your Heart's Content!

In a state recognized as having some of the most wonderful shopping opportunities in the world, Gainesville holds its own here in North Texas. Downtown offers a myriad of wonderful, unique little shops, cafés and specialty stores. Shop for antiques, collectibles, hand crafted art and home furnishings, then enjoy an old-fashioned milkshake or soda for a second wind. From the quaint little shops in the historic downtown area to the major retail centers and outlet malls, Gainesville will surprise you with its value. Gainesville Factory Shops, which opened more than 10 years ago, attracts more than 1.5 million visitors each year. There are holiday sidewalk sales, home and garden shows and monthly exhibits that are very successful. We hope you will enjoy browsing the array of wonderful shops of Gainesville, whether you are searching for something unusual like a piece of South American pottery, or the latest in fashion and jewelry trends. You will find bargains galore, and some of the nicest people in the state. *(Color photo featured in front section of book.)*

For more information about Gainesville, contact the Gainesville Chamber of Commerce at 888-585-4468, 940-665-2831 or visit www.gainesvilletexas.org online.

Gainesville Fairs Festivals & Fun

January
Martin Luther King, Jr. Day
Celebration

February
North Texas Farm Toy Show

March
Medal of Honor Golf
Tournament and Banquet

April
Germanfest
Spring Fling in the Park

May
Antique Car Show
Model Horse Show

June
Texas Chapter of Antique
Airplane Association Annual
Fly-In

July
Rodeo

August
Hunter's Expo and BBQ Cook
Off

September
Australian Shepard Dog Show

October
Common Threads Quilt Show
Depot Day Festival
First United Methodist Table
Top Exhibit
Zoo Boo

November
Arts and Crafts Sell O Rama

December
Holiday Home Tour
Holiday Lighted Parade and
Tree Lighting
Journey to Bethlehem
Victorian Stroll

ANTIQUE & DESIGN CENTER OF NORTH TEXAS

With 50,000 square feet of showroom space, the Antique & Design Center of North Texas is the largest center for antiques and collectibles in North Texas, taking antique shopping to a new level. The Antique & Design Center is located in the circa 1884 Tyler & Simpson Wholesale Grocers building at 502 E. California St. in Gainesville.

The building has quite a history, including one story that draws curious visitors from afar. The story goes like this: long ago a man named "Shorty" was locked in the store cigar vault as a joke. However, his friends left for lunch and drinks, and they completely forgot about their friend. He was left there for eternity. "Shorty the ghost" adds unique excitement and mystery to this antique shopper's paradise. Don't be surprised if you "bump" into him. There are more than 50 dealers represented here featuring antiques, crystal chandeliers, silver, china, clocks, architecturals, artwork, stained glass, rugs and more. The Antique & Design Center of North Texas is conveniently located north of the DFW Metroplex and is open Monday-Saturday 10 am - 5 pm. Plan to spend the entire day if possible; there is so much to explore, and so many wonderful treasures to discover! Who knows...you just might get a glimpse of Shorty! Visit www.adcnt.com online or call 940-665-8847.

MISS PITTYPAT'S ANTIQUE EMPORIUM

The original Gainesville JCPenney department store, built in the early 1920s, has been renovated to reveal the original hardwood floors and gorgeous oak-slatted banisters beneath many layers of paint. Since 1997, the 13,000 square foot historic building, located at 111 W. California St., has been home to Miss Pittypat's Antique Emporium, which specializes in Old English and American furniture, antique glassware, Victorian jewelry, Schaffer pens, fishing lures, Boyd's Bears, and much, much more. You can browse for hours in this wonderful antique heaven, and then enjoy lunch or a cup of tea in Edelweiss TeaHaus, located upstairs on the mezzanine floor. You will love getting to know the owners, Gary and Pam Stillwell, who are very knowledgeable about antiques and collectibles. Miss Pittypat's—we just love the name—is open Monday - Friday 10 am - 5 pm, Saturday until 6 pm and Sunday 1 - 5 pm. Call 940-665-6540 to learn more.

Edelweiss TeaHaus

No matter how busy, folks in Gainesville make time for lunch at Edelweiss TeaHaus on a regular basis. Everything about this charming tearoom is absolutely wonderful. It is located at 111 W. California St. in the upstairs loft of this former 1920s JC Penney Department Store, overlooking Miss Pittypat's Antiques Emporium. Owners Greg and Charla Taylor have created a menu that includes delicious, creative tearoom fare, as well as heartier dishes like German sausage and Rueben sandwiches. And, the portions are large enough to satisfy any husband who has been sweet enough to tag along. The most popular items on the menu include the TeaHaus Salad Platter—with choices of seven delicious salads and homemade dressings—and, of course, the incredible desserts. Naturally, we just had to try several. Will—Greg and Charla's son—makes the best brownies we have ever tasted, but our favorite had to be the Toffee Brownie Trifle! Yum! Edelweiss TeaHaus is open Monday - Saturday 11 am - 4 pm. For more information, call 940-665-6540.

Attractions, Entertainment & Museums

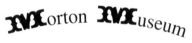 **orton Museum**

OF

COOKE COUNTY

The historic building at 210 S. Dixon St. was erected in 1884 as Gainesville's combination city hall, fire station and calaboose (jail). At that time, it was a visible symbol of the city's growing prosperity, complete with a bell in the tower that rang every night at 9:00 for curfew, and every time there was a fire. Today, the building has been renovated to house the Morton Museum of Cooke County. Visitors to the Morton Museum will see exhibits that portray early life in Gainesville during important periods of history such as the Civil War, cattle drives and WWII, when Camp Howze brought thousands of soldiers to town. The themed exhibits change every two to three months, some revolving around unique facets of Cooke County history, such as: the Gainesville Community Circus, baseball and outlaws. The Morton Museum is open Tuesday-Friday 10 am - 5 pm and Saturday 2 - 5 pm. Call 940-668-8900 or visit www.mortonmuseum.org online.

LEGENDS AND LORE OF GAINESVILLE

Are you a history buff? Then you'll love Gainesville! As you spend time in Gainesville's historic downtown district, you will notice storyboards depicting the history of the town. Legends and Lore of Gainesville is an exciting program providing visitors to downtown the opportunity to learn about the history of each participating building. It encompasses the architectural history, business history and many stories about the early pioneers of the town and the businesses that shaped the future of Gainesville. This unique, self-guided walking tour is filled with interesting photographs and stories that are funny, informative and heartwarming. From the buildings that housed the Gainesville National Bank and Lindsay National Bank to the buildings that were once saloons, you will learn the fascinating histories of each one. Legends and Lore of Gainesville adds the perfect touch of history to a shopping experience that is already incredible. For more information, call 940-668-4530 or 940-668-8900.

Named after the father and pioneer of modern-era zoos, the Frank Buck Zoo, located at 1000 W. California St. in Gainesville, has been serving the children, schools and citizens of North Central Texas and Southern Oklahoma for more than 50 years. Frank Buck was born in Gainesville in 1884, traveled the globe 12 times and crossed the Pacific Ocean 45 times, collecting animals that earned him the nickname, "Bring 'em Back Alive Buck." The zoo is now home to more than 130 animals from four continents of the world, and recently added an exciting "African Savannah" exhibit. The staff at Frank Buck Zoo is dedicated to delivering educational, quality, family-oriented recreation, and the up-close exhibits help visitors get a better view of the animals. The zoo is open daily year-round 9 am - 5 pm, except for Christmas Eve and Day. Educational programs are available Tuesday - Thursday by appointment. For information, call 940-668-4533 or visit www.frankbuckzoo.com online.

SANTA FE DEPOT MUSEUM

A visit to the Santa Fe Depot Museum, 605 E. California St., gives visitors an insight into the significance of transportation during Gainesville's early years. The museum is located in a restored 1902 Santa Fe Depot, which included the Harvey House from 1902–1931. Visitors will see exhibits featuring the Butterfield Stage, cattle drives and the railroad. There is also a special tribute to the Harvey House—a restaurant whose focus was to increase Santa Fe ridership by offering high quality food at reasonable prices for the train traveler, and the Harvey Girls—young ladies trained to serve hundreds of passengers in about 20 minutes...the average length of time a train would need for servicing every four hours. Upstairs, exhibits portray the typical sleeping quarters and uniforms of the Harvey Girls. The Santa Fe Depot Museum also hosts newsreels and artifacts of Gainesville's most celebrated citizens—the Gainesville Community Circus. The circus was born as a fundraiser for the local community theater during the Depression, and by 1936, was universally hailed as one of the greatest shows in the nation. The museum is open Wednesday-Sunday 11 am-2 pm. For more information, call 940-668-8900.

Bed & Breakfasts, Cabins, Cottages & Inns

Donna and Craig Hertel have beautifully transformed one of the oldest homes of historic Gainesville into a spectacular bed and breakfast. Named for their precious daughter, Miss Olivia's is a beautiful Italianate Victorian home located at 319 S. Denton—the tree-lined street just south of the courthouse square. Hardware merchant Mr. William Fletcher built the house in 1882 and installed the finest light fixtures and hardware—many of which have been converted from gas to electricity. In fact, much of the furnishings in the house have fascinating histories, just like the house. Ask Donna about the money found in the wall during a remodel of the kitchen!

Donna is a professional caterer, an event planner and a master gardener, and this project has been her dream come true. Visitors always comment on the warm and welcoming atmosphere, and we'd have to agree. Each of the three guest suites is decorated in rich colors and fantastic fabrics, beautiful antiques and luxurious bedding, and each has a private bath. Guests are treated to a delicious three-course gourmet breakfast extravaganza on the weekends, and a heavy continental breakfast during the week, as well as a sweet surprise with the evening turndown service. You'll love the lavish gardens, the pool, the waterfall and pond, and the magnificent moonlit garden—very romantic. Many brides choose Miss Olivia's for their weddings, where every detail from the food at the reception to the champagne and chocolates in the bridal suite is simply perfect. Visit www.missolivias.com online or call 940-665-5558. *(Color photo featured in front section of book.)*

Alexander
Bed & Breakfast Acres, Inc.
"ABBA"

Nestled peacefully on 65 acres of woods and meadows just 30 minutes from Gainesville at 3692 County Rd. 201. Alexander Bed & Breakfast Acres, Inc.—better known as "ABBA"—is the perfect setting for romantic escapes, small weddings and celebrations, church retreats, or ladies' getaways. Relax on the wrap-around porch or shaded gazebo, sunbathe on the large split-level deck overlooking the pool, or journey along the wooded walking trails that meander through the back woods. ABBA has been a working farm since 1994—so, who knows, you may even be greeted by Cousco, the curious llama or his donkey-friend, Christopher Cross!

Five second-floor bedrooms are appointed in beautiful antiques and luxurious bedding, and the entire third floor is a suite that can be utilized for many occasions. Also, the property offers a darling, three bedroom country Guest House and a one bedroom Country Cottage. Main House rates include a full-country breakfast featuring ABBA's homemade, hot, fresh rolls, as well as refreshments for

"porch-sitting." Come and see for yourself—it is well worth the journey! Contact owners Jimmy and Pamela Alexander at 800-887-8794 or 903-564-7440 for information and availability, or visit www.alexanderbnb.com online.

Books & Soda Fountains

STARRBOOKS

A welcoming sign hangs at the front door of one of the "stars" in Gainesville. It reads, "Through this door walk the finest people . . . our customers. Thank you." Want to escape for an afternoon? Go ahead and walk through those doors. Timothy and Kathie Parks have created the most charming combination of bookstore, soda fountain, gift boutique, and fun, local hangout.

Long-time residents of Gainesville love reminiscing about the "good ole days" spent in the store when it was Watt's Pharmacy. Young and old alike sidle up to the original soda fountain for an old-fashioned shake and a famous "Watt's Chicken Salad Sandwich." The Parks' mission for StarrBooks is to unite book lovers and books! They have a selection of more than 2,000 signed books—local and Texas authors, a large collection of books about early Gainesville and Cooke County, and they specialize in finding out-of-print books for their custom- ers. StarrBooks is located at 103 S. Commerce St. and is open Tuesday- Friday 10 am-5:30 pm and Saturday until 3 pm. Contact the Parks at 940- 612-0202.

Hannah Bananas

When Regina Sturgeon opened this Gainesville upscale children's resale shop at 320-A E. California St., it was in memory of her baby boy Grayson. It also served as an outlet for her grief. Located in the historic Lindsay House Hotel built in 1880, she named the store for her adorable daughter Hannah, who has been an inspiration for the wonderful children's clothing and accessories she carries. You will find fabulous name-brand clothing and toys at incredible prices, so if you love bargains, you will love Hannah Bananas Upscale Children's Resale. The store is open Tuesday-Friday 10 am-5 pm and Saturday until 3 pm. Contact Regina at 940-668-6885.

The Body Garden

Just browsing The Body Garden at 105 W. California St. in Gainesville—this beautiful establishment will inspire relaxation and well-being. This early 1800s building has a Victorian commercial exterior and an interior with displays of heavenly scented bath and body care products that fill the air. Customers' senses are both piqued and soothed with delicious aromas. Owners Karen Barclay and Sue Scofield are constantly changing their inventory to include the latest in beautiful lines of wonderful body care products. They carry The Thymes, Crabtree & Evelyn, Ahava, Archipelago Botanicals and a wide range of lavender products, including a wonderful soap called "La Lavande." You will also find fabulous candles and great clothing lines, including Flax Clothing and PJ Salvage pajamas. Revel in the ancient art of Reflexology as you experience the relaxation and release of stress with their in-house expert Sherry Adelson. The Body Garden is open Monday - Friday 10 am - 5:15 pm and Saturday 10 am - 3 pm. For more information, call 940-665-1100.

Unique Collection, Inc.

Want to dress like a million bucks without breaking the bank? Well, stop by Unique Collection, Inc., 201 W. Broadway, located just off the downtown historic square. Owner Betty West has been dressing the ladies of Gainesville for more than 10 years with fashions that look great but cost a fraction of the retail price. She has both new and consignment apparel and accessories, featuring famous label consignments in excellent condition. You will find a great selection of purses and belts, as well as beautiful jewelry to accessorize any ensemble. Betty gives one word of advice to shoppers, "If you like it, buy it! It is the only one of its kind, and might not be here tomorrow." Browse through this Unique Collection of fabulous designer and famous label clothing that will make you look like a million (for a whole lot less). Shop Tuesday - Friday 10 am - 5:30 pm and Saturday until 4 pm. For more information, call 940-665-2232.

Florists, Gifts & Home Décor

"I am the Vine, you are the branches" John 15:5

Lynn Monden and Peggy Salas chose the name for their store from John 15:5 in the Bible: "I am the vine; you are the branches. If a man remains in me and I in him, he will bear much fruit; apart from me you can do nothing." They give God the glory for their talents, and love using them to help women make their home beautiful. Vine & Branches is located at 107 W. California St. in an historic building just across from the courthouse in Gainesville. Friends for 23 years and partners for more than 15, Peggy and Lynn have built a wonderful reputation for their remarkable floral creations and bridal design expertise. Lynn's daughter Carly Short has also proven to be an excellent floral designer. Best of all, Lynn and Carly make house calls! Vine & Branches is a beautiful place, filled with exquisite flowers, inspirational gifts and a charming atmosphere. Potpourri, candles and home fragrance, along with framed artwork and accessories, provide a wide selection for your home and gift-giving. During the Christmas season, the shop is a wonderland of beauty and unique decorating ideas. The store is open Tuesday-Friday 10 am - 5 pm and Saturday until 3 pm. For more information or consultation, call 940-612-1829.

southwest, ethnic & eclectic

Home Decor & Gifts

Located in an interesting historic Gainesville building at 103 W. California St., Bella Matiz offers customers a unique blend of the Southwest, ethnic and eclectic décor. Owner Mikki Jones has quite an eye for the unusual, with a desire to blend different styles and influences into a living space that feels unpretentious and relaxed. This wonderful mix of "old and new" includes various handmade items and folkart pieces, Root Candles, Burt's Bees products, and jewelry—which is mostly Native American made. Mikki also carries home décor items, including handmade furniture, gorgeous pottery, beautiful rugs and magnificent art. Her ideas will inspire you to look at your surroundings with a new prospective, and you will love discovering the unique, eclectic treasures of "Bella Matiz." The store is open Tuesday-Saturday 10 am - 5 pm. You may contact Mikki at 940-668-8418.

B Hive

Debbie Beauchamp and Carrie Branson absolutely contradict the typical mother-in-law/daughter-in-law stereotype. They are wonderful friends and co-owners of the B Hive, one of the most successful, most sophisticated boutiques in Gainesville. They specialize in wedding registry, personal service and a signature complimentary gift-wrap. You will find the most wonderful lines in unique home décor—from traditional to contemporary. Plus, B Hive carries beautiful, fashion accessories like Brighton and Vera Bradley, as well as the popular line of Tyler candles. The B Hive is a favorite place for groups to gather and shop and, if you call ahead, Carrie and Debbie will have refreshments waiting. Visit the store at 100 W. Main St., Monday through Friday 10 am - 5 pm and Saturday 10 am - 4 pm. For more information, contact the busy "B Hive ladies" at 940-665-8566.

Jewelry

As a retired geology teacher of 20 years, Barbara Inglish's knowledge and love of gems was a natural bridge into the jewelry business. Barron's Fine Jewelry, 101 E. California St. in Gainesville, has been called the "Best Little Jewelry Store in Texas." Located in a historic building dating back to the 1800s, this family-owned-and-operated business has been offering the very best in personal customer service since 1986. Barbara says, "There is absolutely nothing wrong with a woman being high maintenance. That just makes her interesting!" She encourages customers to hold, to touch and to be privy to all of the merchandise and its lore. The cases are filled with an unparalleled selection of exquisite jewelry, but Barron's has become quite famous for its upper-end artisan sterling silver jewelry and 14-karat slide bracelets. Besides a vast array of showcased slides, they will create custom slides from Grandmother's Sweet 16 ring or Uncle Fred's favorite tie pin, making them treasured heirlooms filled with sentiment and memories. Trunk shows and open house days offer fantastic adventures for jewelry lovers. Sometimes out-of-towners come in the morning, break for lunch, and then return in the afternoon in order to see it all! You will find a treasure here. Barron's Fine Jewelry is open Monday - Saturday 10 am - 5 pm. Call 940-665-4223. *(Color photo featured in front section of book.)*

The stellar reputation of Kinne's Jewelers is almost as old as the historic building it has occupied since 1889. Kinne's Jewelers, 210 E. California St., is one of only three jewelers in Texas to be listed in the JA100 Club—Jewelry Stores in America over 100 years old. All of the fixtures and showcases are original to the business, and there is a delightful Mezzanine Museum. Owner Gina Dill has the latest in gemological instrumentation and loves using the local architecture for her design inspiration. She has fine diamonds and precious stones, as well as semi-precious and sterling silver jewelry. You will also find a large selection of Waterford crystal and unique gift items. Kinne's Jewelers is a full-service jewelry store and offers the latest techniques in jewelry craftsmanship. Bench Certified Denny Huggins is on staff to ensure the best possible attention to your jewelry repair. The store is open Monday-Friday 9 am-5 pm, Saturday until noon. Call 940-665-3931. Kinne's Jewelers is a Gainesville historical treasure!

Restaurants

FRIED PIE Co. & RESTAURANT

Fried pies—flaky, crispy dough wrapped around delicious fruit and cream fillings. These individual tantalizing treats have made Jo Clark and the Fried Pie Co. & Restaurant quite famous throughout North Texas. Jo started frying pies in 1980 for friends at home until her husband, who slept days, said enough! She opened her Fried Pie Co. in 1982, at 202 W. Main St. in Gainesville. She now serves breakfast and lunch as well, but folks still come for the pies. In fact, during the holidays the line sometimes wraps around the building! Flavors include apple, cherry, chocolate, peach and blueberry. Don't miss out on the favorite flavors—apricot and coconut. The restaurant is open Monday-Friday 7 am-4:30 pm and Saturday until 3 pm. Call 940-665-7641. Delicious!!

A local hangout, The Main Street Pub and Eatery, is a favorite for Gainesville's locals, and we're sure it will become one of yours, too. It's the perfect place to unwind with a drink after work or enjoy a delicious dinner with friends or family. Located at 216 W. Main St., it is in what used to be a car dealership during the early days of Gainesville. The original tin ceiling and vintage furnishings provide a historical ambiance to this local eatery. Of course, the décor is only the beginning. The food is what will really win your heart—and stomach. The menu features mouth-watering appetizers, like Irish Nachos and Spinach Quesadillas, fresh salads and superb entrees. If you love prime rib, you'll definitely want to visit on Friday or Saturday night to try this featured dish. Or enjoy one of the house specialties: Fresh Rainbow Trout, pan-seared with special seasonings. It's unforgettable! There are also appetizing sides and a generous children's menu. It's a fun place to relax and savor fabulous food, great company, and a slice of Gainesville's history. The Pub is open Monday-Thursday 11 am-11 pm and Friday-Saturday until midnight. For information, call 940-668-4040.

Sarah's Garden Cafe

The folks of Gainesville no longer have to wait for the next party or celebration to be able to enjoy the delicious specialties created by Donna Hertel. Donna has been a caterer in the North Texas area for many years, earning a reputation for quality and creativity. Her restaurant, Sara's Garden Café, 115 W. California St., is a long-awaited event for both Donna and her long-time customers. The café is located in an 1880s-circa building, which was once a brothel and saloon. (Be sure to ask about its "colorful" history!) The décor includes an ornately carved wooden bar, taken from one of the original saloons in Gainesville. Even though Donna now has a charming setting for her delicious food, she will continue to offer catering services to any area location. She is famous for her desserts—cakes, cookies, bars and especially brownies—so be sure to sample her trademark sweets! Chocolate lovers will think they've died and gone to heaven.

The lunch menu includes homemade soups, great salads, sandwiches and pastas—all made with the freshest ingredients and local produce. The evening menu features unique dishes like crawfish fettuccine and rib eye steak covered with thin onion rings. In addition to the mouth-watering fare, unique and creative gift items are available. Gardening enthusiasts will especially love this café and shop. The Café is open Tuesday-Wednesday 11 am-4 pm, Thursday-Friday until 9 pm, Saturday until 10 pm, and is also available for private receptions. For more information, contact Donna at 940-612-5558.

Be sure and check out Babe's Chicken Dinner House at 204 N. 4th St. in Sanger. See pages 78 and 232 for full details.

Terri Baker invites "tired bodies and weary souls" to enter her beautiful Gainesville spa at 113 N. Dixon St., for one of 15 different massages and body treatments. Located in a building that dates back to 1870, Terri opened Essential Kneads in 1997, and has never looked back. Her work as a massage therapist has been fulfilling and meaningful, because she believes that she is truly helping people. Denise Stone joined Terri in 2001—just when the workload was beginning to overwhelm her—and the two have become wonderful friends. They work together in educating their clients on wellness. Essential Kneads offers treatments in Swedish, Deep Tissue, Therapeutic and Hot Stone Massage, as well as Reflexology, Reiki, Polarity Therapy, Myofascia Release, Salt Scrubs and Mud Wraps. Essential Kneads is open Monday - Friday 10 am - 6 pm and Saturday by appointment only. Contact Terri or Denise at 940-665-6046. Custom packages are available and make wonderful gifts!

In the state that prides itself on having more shopping opportunities than anywhere else in the country, there is one place that beckons to serious shoppers with incredible bargains on best-loved brands. Gainesville Factory Shops is located at 4321 I-35 N., Exit 501, and is one of the area's greatest attractions. You will find considerable discounts at more than 55 stores with everything from your favorite fashion lines to home accessories and jewelry. Outlet companies include Mikasa, OshKosh B'Gosh, Zales, Brooks Brothers, Levi's Outlet by MOST, Nike, Kasper, Gap, Naturalizer, VF and Haggar. The Gainesville Factory Shops provide a children's play area, strollers, wheelchairs, ATM machines, a food court (very necessary), and even a full-service RV Park and bus parking. If possible, plan to arrive in time for the very popular "4th Monday Trade Days" at the Factory Shops. There are holiday sidewalk sales and monthly events that help attract more than 1.5 million visitors each year. The stores are open Monday-Saturday 10 am - 8 pm and Sunday 11 am - 6 pm. For information, call 940-668-6092 or visit www.gainesvillefs.com online.

Discover Lewisville

The progressive urban community of Lewisville is located only 20 miles north of downtown Dallas, and 34 miles northeast of downtown Fort Worth. Its excellent location, so close to the DFW International Airport, offers easy access to the Metroplex and the world.

Historical Lewisville

The town of Lewisville was incorporated in 1925, but the settlement actually had its beginnings almost 80 years before. During the 1840s, the Republic of Texas gave a grant to the Texas Emigration and Land Company that would bring 600 families to what is now Denton County. Many settlers began arriving in 1846, and among them were John and James Holford. The Holfords brought several families with them. Thus, the original settlement was called Holford Prairie. In 1855, Mr. Basdeal Lewis bought the Holford land and laid out a town he then named for himself—Lewisville.

When the Wichita Railroad was laid about two miles east of the settlement, the town's activity began to shift in that direction. That section is known today as Lewisville's "Old Town." The community included a scattering of farms, but most of it was located between the present Charles Street and Kealy Avenue, and a block north and south of Main Street. In fact, the site of King's Drug Store in the Lewisville Shopping Center was once a cotton gin.

Although Lewisville is now a city of 88,000, its population was only 1,500 as late as 1950. The corps of engineers changed everything with the construction of the Lewisville Lake Dam in

1954. After the dam was built, unprecedented home building began during the 1970s, with entire neighborhoods springing up almost overnight. During the 1980s and 1990s, Lewisville was identified as an "employment center"—which accounts for its tremendous growth up to this point.

Fun in Lewisville

Of course you can take advantage of all that Dallas and Fort Worth have to offer so close by, but before you do, make sure you take time to enjoy Lewisville. The 29,000-acre Lake Lewisville has 233 miles of shoreline, and is deep enough for all types of water sports. Families enjoy boating, skiing, sailing and fishing. You can also explore the miles of scenic trails around the lake.

Shopping is top notch here, with continued improvements and renovations, especially at Old Town Lewisville. Many of the charming storefronts date from the turn of the century. You'll find boutiques, specialty shops and wonderful restaurants. While in Old Town, be sure to visit The Feed Mill—an anchor in Old Town since the 1800s. Here you will be surrounded by old pieces of farm equipment and household items from the 19th century.

There are also several wonderful antique malls within the Lewisville area, providing hours and hours of browsing fun. Go ahead—shop 'til you drop! *(Color photo featured in front section of book.)*

For additional information about Lewisville, contact the Lewisville Chamber of Commerce and Visitors Bureau at 972-436-9571, 800-657-9571 or visit www.lewisville-chamber.org or www.visitlewisville online.

Lewisville Fairs Festivals & Fun

May
Cinco de Mayo Fiesta
Sounds of Lewisville Summer Concert Series (May-July)

July
Dog Days of Summer Dog Show
Family Concert in the Park
July 4th Children's Parade
Red, White and Lewisville Fireworks and Festival

August
Highland Village Balloon Festival

September
Labor Day Rodeo
Sounds of Lewisville Fall Concert Series (Sept-Oct)
Western Days in Old Town Lewisville

October
Lebanese Food Festival

November
Holiday Arts and Crafts Fair

December
Holiday at the Hall Festival

Antiques

"We want you to feel like you've stepped back in time," say owners Joe and Selva Casas. They have created a unique store that caters to just about any decorating style you can imagine. From formal traditional to eclectic art deco, you will find treasures for every room of your home—antique furniture from the 1800s to the 1950s, vintage and contemporary linens, works of art and collectibles, including: Fenton Art Glass, Blenko Art Glass, Anheuser-Busch Steins and much more. You'll be amazed by the wonderful collectible costume and fine estate jewelry selections! String of Pearls, 123-127 W. Main St. in Old Town Lewisville, is an antique lovers dream come true! Open Monday-Saturday 10:30 am-5:30 pm. Call 972-353-5033..

GREATER LEWISVILLE COMMUNITY THEATRE

 If you are looking to inject your life with a little culture, the Greater Lewisville Community Theatre is just the ticket. Currently in its 21st year, the theatre has succeeded in bringing lively and engaging performances. In 1997, the Community Theatre purchased its current home at 160 W. Main St. in Lewisville and has provided the area with superior entertainment at affordable prices ever since. For the last five seasons, it has featured the best of contemporary and traditional comedy, drama and musical theatre. The Greater Lewisville Community Theatre is also proud to award annual scholarships to Lewisville Independent School District seniors, who will pursue college degrees in the theatre arts. For tickets or information, call 972-221-SHOW (7469) or visit www.glct.org online.

 Organized in 1978, The Visual Art League's small group of members sought to enhance the appreciation of artistic talent in Lewisville. To accomplish this, classes and workshops for art instruction and exhibitions were held by professional artists. The Visual Art League is made up of artists, art educators and others who have a passion for visual art. Its work is more important today than ever before. The Visual Art League's Art Center, 701 S. Stemmons Fwy., can be utilized for artist exhibitions, receptions, workshops and classes dedicated to the visual arts. The Center is open Thursday-Saturday 1-4 pm. For appointment call 972-420-9393 or visit www.visualartleague.org online.

LEWISVILLE LAKE SYMPHONY

The Lewisville Lake Symphony is regarded as one of the best regional symphony orchestras in Texas. Led by Maestro Adron Ming, the Symphony, 1301 W. Hwy 407, was founded in 1984, and has thrived due in large part to the support of locals  who love everything from Beethoven and Mozart to works by contemporary American composers. The Symphony's mission—"to excite the brain, and nourish the soul"—is evident in their challenge to involve the young people of Lewisville with local competitions and opportunities to perform as guests. To learn more about the wonderful performances, visit www.lewisvillesymphony.org online or call 972-874-9087.

Bridal, Weddings & Catering

The Orndorf Haus

From the beautiful fountain outside to the simple elegant motif inside, you will appreciate the cozy yet elegant atmosphere of The Orndorf Haus as you plan your wedding or social event. Janice Orndorf, elected to the national registry of Who's Who in the U.S.A. in Catering and Floral Design and celebrating 28 years of quality service to the Metroplex, is now available to meet your catering and floral needs at The Orndorf Haus in Highland Village.

Janice personally designs each function to fit each client's needs, desires and budget. With her fully trained professional staff and four-star service, Janice offers catering on or off the premises. Located at 2300 Highland Village Rd., #900, The Orndorf Haus is open for consultations by appointment only Monday-Friday. For more information, call 972-317-2632 or visit www.orndorfhaus.com online.

Bridal Boutique

Out of the ordinary—into the uncommon. That's what you'll find at Bridal Boutique, 119 W. Main St., in historic downtown Lewisville. Open since 1990, Bridal Boutique provides personal customer service in intimate comfortable surroundings. You will find more than 300 different gowns affordably priced. From bridal gowns to prom dresses, Bridal Boutique has the perfect ensemble for your special occasion. Outstanding customer service, friendly helpful staff, and truly the best selection you'll find anywhere. No appointment is necessary, so stop by Monday, Tuesday, Wednesday and Friday 10 am - 6 pm, Thursday until 7 pm, Saturday until 5 pm and Sunday 1 - 5 pm. For more information, call 972-219-8500 or visit online at www.bridalboutiquelewisville.com.

No man or woman is worth your tears,
and the one who is, won't make you cry.

— Unknown

Second Home Furniture

This family business, owned and operated by Stacy Van Cleve, offers quality new and used furniture and home décor at great values. Customers say the relaxing music, enjoyable atmosphere and friendly staff make this shop very unique. You'll even find hand-picked iron import pieces at great prices. Second Home Furniture, open 10 am - 6 pm Monday-Saturday, is located at 1288 W. Main St. #132 in Lewisville. For more information, call 214-222-HOME (4663).

Added Touches
Specialty Gift Shop

Cathy Groves had always loved shopping in this cute gift boutique at 122 W. Main in Old Town Lewisville, so when she heard that the owner was retiring, she thought it such a shame for the town to lose this treasure. So, she bought it. Today, Cathy continues the tradition of carrying the finest in collectibles and home décor. The window displays in this circa 1920s building are inviting collections of seasonal decorative items, goodies and gifts. She carries Precious Moments, Collegiate, Angels Among Us and Ty Products, as well as a large selection of candles and personal care products. Cathy and her staff are so friendly you will want to stay to enjoy a cup of cappuccino. Added Touches is open Monday-Wednesday 10 am - 6 pm, Thursday until 5 pm, Friday until 7 pm and Saturday 9 am - 5 pm. For more information, call 972-436-3161 or visit www.addedtouches.net.

Gardens & Nurseries

Hartwell's Nursery, 1570 N. Stemmons Expwy., has blossomed since 1964 into a premier Lewisville garden shop—it is a garden lover's paradise! Stop by Monday-Friday 8:30 am-6 pm, Saturday until 5 pm and Sunday 10 am-4 pm. To learn more, call 972-436-3612 or visit www.hartwellsnursery.com.

Gourmet, Specialty Foods & Restaurants

Dallas Tortilla & Tamale Factory

With the help of her husband, mother and father, Rebecca Leal Behnke opened a small space in Old Town Lewisville to serve hot tamales and tortillas made famous by her grandmother Elvira Portugal Leal.

Elvira started making tortillas in her mother's kitchen, while waiting for her husband Ruben to come back from World War II. She began selling tortillas to neighbors, and with her family's encouragement, opened a tortilla factory in Dallas. Elvira soon had enough money to buy some land in what was known as Little Mexico—this became the site of their first Dallas Tortilla Factory. When Ruben returned from the war, not only did he find that his wife was selling her tortillas, he met his first of four sons for the very first time! The entire Leal family has worked hard over the years and has expanded their menu to include tamales and many traditional Mexican dishes.

Today, granddaughter Rebecca carries on a tradition that began with her grandmother. These delicious handmade tortillas and tamales are still made the old-fashioned way. Starting with stone-ground corn and filled with pork, chicken or beef, the Leal Family keeps the tradition alive. The tamales are so good, they have even made their way to the White House! The factory is located at 310 S. Mill St., and hours vary during the different seasons. Call 972-436-4333 or visit www.hottamaleez.com online to place your order—lines form early during the holidays!

OLD TOWN MARKET

D Magazine calls this Lewisville Old Town Market, 301 S. Mill St., one of the "Best Meat Markets in Dallas." The Food Network has featured owners Dickie and Lou Grant and daughter Marsha on an episode of "Food 911." Will all of this publicity change the way Dickie Grant does business? Not at all. Old Town Market has been a local favorite for 28 years, so Dickie's customers are not at all surprised at the "prime time" press. It is a family-owned, old-fashioned meat market where customers come in to stock up on choice cuts of beef, pork, poultry and shop-made sausages. The entire family works overtime during the holidays preparing smoked hams, turkeys, prime rib roast and beef tenderloin. The Market is also a favorite place for lunch, which is served Tuesday-Saturday 11 am-2 pm. Everything is absolutely delicious! Don't forget Old Town Market when planning your holiday party. For information and catering, call 972-436-6742. The Market is open Tuesday-Friday 7:30 am-6 pm and Saturday until 5 pm.

Mama Norma has been serving homemade pies, cornbread, rolls and good ol' home cooking for more than 45 years, so it is no surprise that Mama's daughters picked up lessons along the way. Daughter, Laurie Bowers, owns and operates the Lewisville location of Mama's Daughters' Diner, 1288 W. Main St. #160, where long-time customers know they will always find the best home cooking in town. From hearty breakfasts like Biscuits and Gravy with Sausage and Ham to favorite lunchtime specials like Chicken Fried Steak or Chicken and Dumplings, just to name a few. Everything is homemade and delicious! Don't miss the cream and fruit pies, as well as the delicious cobblers. Be sure to check out the other Mama's Daughters' Diners in Dallas at 2610 Royal Ln. and 2014 Irving Blvd., in Irving at 2412 W. Shady Grove, and in Mesquite at 2015 N. Galloway. The Diner is open Monday-Saturday 6 am-8 pm. Call 972-353-5955.

HOMEWOOD SUITES®

Hilton

The newly renovated, award-winning Homewood Suites by Hilton offers visitors all the comforts and conveniences of home in beautiful French Country surroundings. One and two bedroom suites feature two separate telephone lines and free wireless high speed Internet access, as well as kitchens equipped with a microwave, full-size refrigerator, dishwasher, cooktop stove, coffee maker and dining area. Business travelers will appreciate the Executive Center with color copier, scanner and computer. On-site laundry and valet service are also available.

Homewood Suites in Lewisville is special because it is family-owned-and-operated. The Shinn family has been in the hotel industry for more than 30 years, so they understand the importance of setting high standards and giving personal attention to their guests. Every care has been taken to ensure your utmost comfort in beautiful rooms. You will even find prints from the Dallas Museum of Art adorning the walls.

You will feel right at home each Monday-Thursday evening at the "Manager's Reception"—a light meal which includes wine, beer and soft drinks. A complimentary buffet breakfast, including meat and egg items, is served each morning, and your morning newspaper is free! You might want to spend the day enjoying the beautifully landscaped swimming pool, hot tub and sport court, or take the complimentary shuttle to one of the many great shopping areas of the city. However you choose to spend the day, you'll love coming "home" at the end of the day to this beautiful place. Homewood Suites is located at 700 Hebron Pkwy. For information or reservations, call 972-315-6123, 800-CALL-HOME or visit www.magnolialodging.com online.

BEASLEY'S JEWELRY

What started as a small jewelry business in 1948 has grown through four generations to be a Lewisville tradition and favorite jewelry store. Martha Zuspan and her daughter Lisa Dubberley carry on the tradition of Beasley's excellence with beautiful items like rings by Hidalgo, 18K and enamel jewelry by Soho, Swiss watches by Maurice LaCroix, and much more. What makes this such a unique jewelry store is that it also doubles as a soda shop! The life-size lion and leopard, and deer head mounts were Norman Zuspan's hunting trophies that entertain young and old alike as they enjoy a delicious old-fashioned soda, milkshake or Coke float! Beasley's Jewelry, 177 W. Main St., is open Monday through Friday 10 am-6 pm and Saturday until 5 pm. Call 972-221-4641.

Quilt Country

 With more than 8,500 bolts of beautiful fabric, quilters (beginner to expert) will find the perfect one for their creation. Quilt Country, 701 S. Stemmons #260 is a premier quilt shop that has been featured in the *Better Homes and Gardens Quilt Sampler Magazine.* Owner Sandy Brawner specializes in batiks, but also carries brights, conversationals, pastels and seasonal fabrics. Quilt Country in Lewisville is the North Texas "Threadquarters" with more than a dozen different types of thread, special needles, stabilizers and yarn embellishers. The store's 12 foot ceiling offers space to display more than 250 models to inspire customers with ideas about style and color. Be sure to check out the class schedule. Open Monday-Saturday 10 am-5 pm and Sunday 1-5 pm. For more information, call 972-436-7022 or visit www.quiltcountry.com online.

LARRY'S
SHOOTING SUPPLIES, INC.

Okay Ladies, just promise them a day at Larry's Shooting Supplies, and your guys might not even mind the rest! This unique Lewisville shop, located at 190 W. Main St., has a warm, comfortable atmosphere where visitors can enjoy a good cup of coffee, swap a story or two, or even enjoy a game of dominoes. Shooters will find an impressive collection of the best guns on the market, including Savage, Remington, Benelli and Berretta, as well as a large section of reloading supplies. Owner Larry Pockrus had been working in gun shops for more than 35 years when he decided to open his own shop. He sharpened his gunsmithing skills at the Kreighoff School for Gunsmiths in Florida. In fact, Larry is considered the best in his field for repair on all types of guns—old and new. The store is open Monday-Friday 9 am-6 pm and Saturday 8 am-5 pm. Visit www.larrysshootingsupplies.com online or call 972-434-0403.

Sports & Fitness

EAGLE POINT MARINA
Lake Lewisville

This family owned, full-service marina, located at 1 Eagle Point Rd. on Lake Lewisville, offers everything you need for a great boating experience. There are more than 700 boat slips for water storage, 230 covered dry storage slips, gated entry and a 24-hour member-only boat ramp. Eagle Point Marina offers a reliable service and parts department, gas dock, boat sales office, as well as private restrooms and showers. The fun restaurant, sports bar and banquet facility, "Sneaky Pete's," overlooks the marina. Outside pools, a gazebo, volleyball courts and banquet rooms are also available. The marina is open Tuesday-Saturday 8:30 am - 5:30 pm. For more information call 972-436-6561 or visit www.eaglepointmarina.com online.

Discover McKinney

McKinney is said to be a "world away" from the hustle and bustle of city life. With its beautiful and thriving Courthouse Square, magnificent historic homes and exciting outdoor activities, it is a top destination for visitors to the Lone Star State. The city possesses a "turn-of-the-century charm" that has earned it a listing in the National Register of Historic Places, boasting of many historical markers. Here's an interesting historical tidbit. Bonnie and Clyde and the notorious Frank and Jesse James used to frequent McKinney! Guess they found the shopping great too! (Or was it the bank?) *(Color photo featured in front section of book.)*

Historical McKinney

The first settlers found their way to this area from Kentucky, Tennessee and Arkansas around 1841. Five years later, the First Texas Legislature created Collin County out of the Territory of Fannin County. The city and county was named for Mr. Collin McKinney, a pioneer, land surveyor and legislator who actually helped draft and later signed the Texas Declaration of Independence. McKinney was incorporated for the first time in 1848, and by 1850 had a population of 315.

McKinney has seen both boom and bust during its history—the latest being the industrial growth of the 1970s and then the real estate and bank busts of the 1980s. With lots of hard work, determination and never-give-up community spirit, McKinney was recently named the fastest growing city in the United States. The downtown square bustles with shoppers and tourists, and new businesses continue to experience exciting growth.

There are more than 3,375 historic structures in McKinney, including the historic Collin County Courthouse, the Collin County Museum, and the Chestnut Square Historical Park. Around the courthouse and throughout the downtown square, you'll find more than 100 antique, boutique and specialty shops to explore and enjoy. Historic McKinney is a wonderful blend of old and new—a small-town community with a big heart.

Chestnut Square Historical Park

This incredible tribute to McKinney's historical importance began as the vision of a small group of women in 1973. Their first project was a Christmas tour of some of the historical homes, which enabled them to purchase the Dulaney cottage and home on Chestnut Street. Today, Chestnut Square Historical Park is a collection of seven buildings restored and maintained to preserve the architecture and history of McKinney and Collin County. Through this unique museum village, visitors from around the world are now able to gain an insight into the lives of those spirited pioneers who first settled the area.

The village tour includes the 1860s Taylor House, which earned the nickname "Two-Bit Taylor Inn." (For two bits, or 25 cents, travelers could sleep on a cot in the attic and eat breakfast in the dining room.) The Johnson House, circa 1874, is a folk-Victorian house featuring a gasoline-powered iron, water-well and storm cellar. The Dulaney cottage, built in 1875 for a prosperous doctor, was one of the first Chestnut Street houses and contains period pieces from many Collin County families. The tour also takes you through the 1908 Chapel, the 1918 Dixie's Grocery Store, the Faires House, 1853, the oldest house in McKinney and the Dulaney House, circa 1916. History buffs will be happy to know that a one-room school—complete with authentic desks and vintage textbooks—will be completed and added to the tour in 2005. This was the only Chestnut Square house to be built with electricity and running water. The entire park is such an incredible experience. You will truly feel as though you have wandered back in time to early America.

Outdoor McKinney

If you can tear yourself away from the incredible shops, eateries and museums, you'll find a beautiful green and colorful world to explore. During the summer, the streets will be lined with vibrant colors of the beautiful Crape Myrtle. The abundance of these beauties in McKinney has prompted the development of the Crape Myrtle Trails Foundation as a civic beautification effort. The foundation's hope is to see "The World Collection of Crape Myrtles" in all public areas of the city. This would consist of all known species and varieties of crape myrtles in public area plantings. Mr. Neil Sperry, one of the state's foremost gardening experts and a founding member of the Crape Myrtle Trails board says, "The Crape Myrtle Trails could become similar to the Azalea Trail in Tyler."

Outdoor enthusiasts can take advantage of 21 parks and five recreational facilities, where they can enjoy everything from horseshoes to camping. The Heard Natural Science Museum and Wildlife Sanctuary has more than four miles of nature trails, natural science exhibits and bird watching. And, the Towne Lake Recreation area features a lake, trails, picnic pavilions and playgrounds.

If flea markets are "your thing," don't miss Third Monday Trade Days, one of the largest flea markets in North Texas. Third Monday continues the tradition of the old countywide markets that were held early on when the Circuit Judge came to McKinney on the third Monday of each month. They have been a huge success in McKinney since 1966. Shoppers browse where Indian teepees once were pitched, on some of the most historic real estate in Texas. There are more than 700 vendors with antiques, collectibles, gifts, home/yard décor, crafts and food. It is a wonderful day, and a great opportunity to find wonderful treasures.

Historic Town Square

Mention the name McKinney and extraordinary shopping comes to mind. There are more than 100 antique, boutique and home-sweet-home shops throughout the brick-lined town square where you can find everything from posh pillows and luxurious throws to chunky jewelry and flowergirl dresses. Designers will love finding architectural-salvage pieces and stained glass, and avid gardeners will find must-have garden and yard essentials. When you tire of shopping, (is there such a thing?) you'll love visiting the soda fountain bar for an old-fashioned shake or a fabulous Frito pie. McKinney has been called, "A Girl's Town." We would have to agree. It's a favorite place for ladies on a "day out," a shoppers paradise and one of our favorites!

For more information about McKinney, contact the McKinney Chamber of Commerce at 972-542-0163 or visit www.mckinneytx.org online. Or, contact the McKinney Tourism Services at 214-544-1407 or visit www.visitmckinney.com online.

McKinney
Fairs Festivals & Fun

May
   Cinco de Mayo Celebration
   Farmers Market (May-October)

June
   Battle of the Bands

July
   Forever Free Celebration

August
   Ice Cream Crank Off

September
   Heard Museum Birds of Prey Festival
   United Tour Texas Bike Race

October
   Scare on the Square

November
   Dickens of a Christmas
   Victorian Christmas at the Heard Museum

December
   Heritage Guild Holiday Tour of Homes

Antiques

Antique House

"An antique shop with *real* antiques," is a comment owner Jean Williams of Antique House, 212 E. Louisiana in McKinney, often hears. After 26 years in business, Jean is proud to offer unusual American and English antiques to her customers. Specializing in 19th- and early 20th-century furniture and English and Continental Majolica, Antique House helps discriminating collectors, as well as newcomers, discover the perfect find. Open 10 am - 5 pm Tuesday-Saturday. Call 972-562-0642.

Mother-daughter owners Dale Roberts and Cindy Wangler of "It Spoke To Me" offer an ever-changing array of eclectic, whimsical and very girly items, including Mark Roberts limited edition fairies, Vicki Carroll dishes, and much more. Just as much as the inventory in their shop has *spoken* to them, we're sure it will speak to you, too. "It Spoke To Me," 103 E. Virginia, #108 inside The Ritz in McKinney, is open 10 am - 5 pm Tuesday-Friday and Saturday 10 am-6 pm. Call 214-544-7131.

THE ANTIQUE COLLECTION

This is a marvelous little antique mall filled with uniques and antiques from top to bottom—a graceful blending of English Cottage, Primitives and Victoriana. The Antique Collection, 112 E. Louisiana St. in McKinney, has been voted one of the top two favorite antique stores in all of Collin County, and it's easy to see why! Owner Karen Dawkins has a real talent for displaying the beautiful "antique collections" so that you can easily imagine these treasures in your own home. Well-styled vignettes showcase beautiful vintage linens, handmade quilts, lovely hooked rugs, textiles and architectural elements, as well as beautiful estate jewelry, china, silver and crystal. Stop by Monday through Friday 10 am-5 pm, Saturday until 5:30 pm and Sunday 1-5 pm. For more information, call 972-529-6994. Estate liquidation, lectures and seminars are available upon request.

Artists & Art Galleries

Located in historical downtown McKinney, the Anthurium Art Gallery, a compendium of colorful artisans, is the brainchild of owner/artist Debra Powell. The Anthurium hosts artwork from more than 50 different local artists—offering oil, acrylic, watercolor, pencil, ceramics, stained glass and jewelry. Just off the square on the southwest side, you'll see beautifully crafted metal sculptures out in front and stained glass in the windows welcoming you into a smorgasbord of fine art. Housed in a 100-year-old building, this remarkable art gallery is the right choice for purchasing fantastic pieces of art to add to your collection.

Located at 105 W. Louisiana St. in McKinney, the Anthurium also offers art classes—summer, after-school and Saturdays for children and by appointment for adults. Stop by 10 am-5 pm Tuesday-Saturday and 1-5 pm Sunday. For more information, call 972-548-0552 or visit www.anthuriumart.com.

Books

Just One More Chapter...

Monica Pulliam says that the very first time she walked into her Junior High School library she knew that one day she would own her own bookstore. She loves books, and she loves having a wonderful place where others can enjoy them, too. Just One More Chapter, located at 116 S. Tennessee St. in McKinney's downtown square, is a charming, cozy store, filled with a large selection of books, totes and sweet gifts. Choose a favorite book, grab a rocking chair, and enjoy the peaceful ambiance as you finish "just one more chapter!" Monica will search for out-of-print books for a small fee, order new books for customers at a 20 percent discount, and encourages customers to bring in used books for credit—which helps local teachers stock their yearly reading material. Just One More Chapter is a member of the "Bookstores That Care" program with *Romantic Times Magazine* in New York and Monica loves being able to support local authors and their new books. The store is open Monday-Saturday 10 am - 5 pm. Call 214-585-4966.

The Little RED HEN

You can't miss the huge "Little Red Hen" that adorns the building at 105 E. Virginia St. in McKinney. She beckons you to "come in for coffee and find a treasure!" Owner Carolyn McGown also reminded us of the fable about The Little Red Hen who says to everyone, "I'll do it myself, and did!" That was her inspiration as she and her husband renovated the circa 1875 building in 1995. It won "Best Historical Renovation" by Texas Downtown Association and The Award of Excellence by the McKinney Chamber of Commerce. Inside you'll find Flax Brand linen clothing and Naot shoes—both exclusive to The Little Red Hen—as well as the most wonderful selection of gifts, antiques, jewelry and Christmas treasures. Hours are Monday-Saturday 10 am - 5:30 pm and Sunday 1 - 5 pm. Call 972-542-0429.

❤ Cotton Hearts ❤

When asked about their favorite places to shop in McKinney, locals always include Dorie Helsley's wonderful clothing and accessory shop Cotton Hearts, 103 E. Virginia #102. You will love the fun, "hip" casual Californian line called Allen Allen, and the large selection of unique T-shirts from lace to cotton. It's no wonder Cotton Hearts has been featured in *Southern Living Magazine* twice! Stop by Monday-Saturday 10 am - 5 pm. Call 972-562-9006.

CYNTHIA ELLIOT
BOUTIQUE, INC.

Cynthia and Steve VanLandingham took a leap of faith in 1993 when they bought and renovated their historic building at 107 E. Virginia St. on McKinney's historic square. They built a "loft area" where they lived above the store and became affectionately known as the "square keepers." They were instrumental in bringing life back to the

downtown area, especially with the success of Cynthia's Boutique. Cynthia says, "I shop till I drop at Market, so you don't have to," and carries clothing and accessories for all occasions. You'll find more than 60 designer lines such as: Joseph Ribkoff, Muse, Susan Bristol and Sharon Young, to name a few. Her assortment of darling novelty handbags is fantastic. The boutique is open Monday-Saturday 10 am-5 pm. Call 972-562-8004.

c.j. riley & co.

At C. J. Riley & Co., 109 S. Tennessee off the square in downtown McKinney, you'll find fabulous home décor and accent furniture pieces to fun and funky women's fashions and "girl stuff." Specializing in cowgirl chic clothing, this unique shop offers a rainbow of cool colors in hand-tooled leather mules and boots. Don't miss the one-of-a-kind jewelry, wall prints, crystal chandeliers, mosaic tiled birdbaths or garden accessories! Open 10 am-5 pm Monday-Saturday. Call 972-562-1896.

Gifts, Home Décor & Interior Design

From the moment you walk through the door of this remarkable McKinney shop, you will be seduced by what the owner calls her "romantic, European, eclectic" style. From the cream colored, sheer panels suspended from the ceiling, to the delicious aroma of her signature candle in the air, Misty Wiebold has created a unique blend of modern, period and exotic furnishings that will add the perfect "dazzle" to your rooms.

Misty started a design business after college, and then decided to open a side business in an antique mall. Her tiny booth soon became extremely popular, and people began to recognize her logo. Due to its continued growth, French Dressing has now settled into its third location at 213 N. Kentucky—a 100-year-old building on McKinney's historic square.

French Dressing offers a full range of design services, distinctive décor, antiques, accessories and custom designed furnishings. This beautiful store is a tasteful departure from the exhausted cookie-cutter looks of today. Misty believes that your décor should be a reflection of "who you are," and French Dressing holds true to this concept. She says, "I have always lived out of my imagination, and have never been a slave to trends." Her style is totally unexpected! You will find a balanced contrast of beautiful elements, a pairing of old and new, wood and metal, exotic and classic, and the result is magnificent. You will also find unique items such as oversized architectural pieces, beautiful lighting and antique chairs covered in chic Parisian fabrics. Be sure to take home one of her exclusive, hand-poured candles called French Dressing "Deux." The shop is open Tuesday-Saturday 10 am - 5 pm. For more information, call 972-547-4416.

We loved the name, the people, and, of course, every single item in the store! Ambrosia Vintage Vogue, 201 E. Virginia St., will become one of your favorite places to shop in McKinney. Nancy Chesser, daughter Amber Heintz, and son Clay Chesser have worked together since 1998

decorating for residential and commercial clients, and finally opened their own store May of 2003. The shop carries unusual antiques, furniture, garden accessories and more! Their special "niche" is called Texas Ranch Romance—rustic with lace! And, they are very excited about a new line called Market #9—one-of-a-kind purses, tassels, pillows and hats. Ambrosia Vintage Vogue is open Monday-Saturday 10 am - 5 pm. For more information, call 972-548-3950.

Restaurants

The beautifully renovated historic house at 107 S. Church St. in McKinney was magically transformed into a wonderful, intimate little restaurant called the Sweet Tomato Garden Café. The idea for this wonderful place came to be when corporate businessman and renovation expert Don Day met Chef Anthony "Tony" Guercio, who just happened to be searching for a restaurant. The combination of their talents culminated in the very successful Sweet Tomato Café! The *Dallas Morning News* says, "The menu is unpretentious and inexpensive, but fresh ingredients, skilled preparation, and sophisticated little touches make this place special!" We loved the Sweet Tomato Deluxe Salad! The fried pickles have even won the Best of Big D Award for Best Addiction! Hours are Monday 11 am-2 pm, Tuesday-Thursday until 9 pm, Friday-Saturday until 10 pm and Sunday 10 am-2 pm. For more information, call 972-562-8386. *(Color photo featured in front section of book.)*

Gifts Etc., located in historical downtown McKinney at 103 E. Virginia, offers wonderfully unique, personalized gift baskets. Carol Edwards' goal in creating her custom-made gift baskets has always been "good quality, affordable pricing and great presentation." She carries gourmet food and candy lines, as well as spectacular balloon arches, sculptures and centerpiece creations. Gifts Etc. is open Monday-Saturday 10 am-5 pm. For more information, call 972-562-5700.

Old Fashioned Pharmacy
Quality Service

People come from miles around just to get a glimpse of this true "Texas Treasure" in McKinney. Smith Drug Co. is the oldest independent pharmacy in all of Texas, and has been at 114 N. Tennessee St., since its beginning in 1859! Kaylei Mosier, only the third owner of Smith Drug Company, offers old-fashioned pharmacy service and a small-town friendly atmosphere. Hours are Monday-Friday 8 am-5 pm and until noon on Saturday. Call 972-542-4431.

Discover
Plano / Frisco / Allen

PLANO

We thought you might like to know that the city of Plano has been ranked sixth by *Ladies' Home Journal* as one of America's 10 Best Cities for Women. We weren't a bit surprised. It is a beautiful city, which has combined its heritage and history with its progressive future in a way that affords both residents and visitors a wonderful experience. Other accolades for Plano include the "Fifth Most Kid Friendly City," and "11th Fastest-Growing City in the U.S. For Cities Over 100,000." Plano was chartered as a Home Rule City in 1961, and designated an All-American City in 1994. *"D" Magazine* named it one of the "Best Places in the Metroplex" to live, and it is listed in the book, "50 Fabulous Cities to Raise A Family."

This thriving, fast-growing community—which boasts award-winning schools, beautiful, spacious parkland and superior transportation system—continues to garner compliments for its quality of lifestyle and opportunities for economic development.

Early Plano

Many attempts were made to settle this area as early as 1841, but Indian attacks thwarted most of the efforts until 1844. One of the early settlers, Mr. William Foreman, built a sawmill and gristmill, which helped the community survive. Later a store and gin were added. Mr. Foreman rejected the idea of naming the town "Foreman," so local doctor Henry Dye suggested the name "Plano," which described the surrounding terrain in Spanish. In the last years of the 1850s, Plano's growth was steady, but the arrival of the Civil War halted everything. After struggling for many years, Plano was infused with new life upon the completion of the Houston and Texas Railroad in 1872. It was the first depot by rail entering Collin County, and almost anything could be bought or traded in Plano. Throughout much of the century, agriculture and farming made up the majority of the business, but with the incredible growth of Dallas during the early 1960s, Plano welcomed newcomers and new businesses at an unprecedented rate.

Fun In Plano!

How about this itinerary for fun? Plano has 80 park sites, 40 miles of recreational hiking trails, three exceptional private golf courses and two public courses, 81 tennis courts and six recreation centers. There are 20 cultural arts organizations including theater, music and ballet. And the shopping is wonderful! Two regional malls, 70 shopping centers and many charming freestanding specialty shops feature wonderful antiques, children's items, arts and crafts, and tearooms. The historic downtown area of Plano has been beautifully preserved and revitalized, including the original storefronts and Victorian homes.

If possible, try to plan your trip to Plano during the fall, because the Hot Air Balloon Festival lifts off in September and it is a wonder to behold. Hundreds of brilliant, colored balloons are launched from Plano, which is the "Hot Air Balloon Capital of Texas."

FRISCO

It is home to the Fujitsu Transaction Solutions, GE Capital, EDS Telecom, as well as the regional office for Levi Strauss and Budweiser. Frisco is one of the fastest growing cities in North Texas, and it's fast becoming one of its major shopping destinations. In fact, according to the 2000 census, Frisco has experienced a 449 percent growth rate since 1990! Wow! Along with its unprecedented population growth, Frisco has also seen incredible commercial growth in the areas of retail, office, industry and technology. New resort hotels, a downtown civic district and impressive shopping make Frisco quite an exciting city. But, even with all of its urban business development at center stage, Frisco has managed to retain one of its most important traits—its country charm. With the opening of the Frisco Heritage Park in late 2005, it will be one of the best places to learn about the town's history, with the preservation of many of the historical buildings and homes from the early days.

Early Frisco

Although the official town of Frisco dates back to 1902, the city's earliest history can be traced to the very early 1800s. When the Congress of the Republic of Texas set aside money for the construction of a north-south road which would open northern Texas to trade, the road ran right through the heart of what would eventually be called Frisco. The road was called the Shawnee Trail, but later became known as Preston Trail, then Preston Road. Just further south on the old Preston Trail is where John Neely Bryan began the "tiny" settlement of Dallas! Transportation has also played a tremendous part in the growth of Frisco. In fact, the railroad became a catalyst for the creation of Frisco when the St. Louis-San Francisco railroad came through the area. A depot was built at the end of Main Street, and the "Frisco Line" made its first stop in 1902. The land, which was incorporated into the City of Frisco was originally owned by the Blackland Townsite Company, a subsidiary of the Frisco Railroad. When an auction for lots was offered to settlers in 1902, it drew residents and merchants from as far away as Chicago, St. Louis and Kansas City.

The charming little country town of Frisco grew slowly but

steadily through the years, but the population explosion of the 1990s catapulted the town into a vibrant city with ever-expanding opportunities. It celebrated its 100th birthday in 2002 with the hope that as large as the city becomes, it never loses its small-town, friendly atmosphere. The city's leaders push toward the future with a united wish—that Frisco will remain "a city with the heart of a town."

Fun in Frisco

Art, golf, world-class sporting events and fabulous city parks—Frisco has it all. Sports enthusiasts have plenty to cheer about as the Texas Tornado hockey team takes the ice in the new Dr Pepper StarCenter. The center holds two sheets of playing ice—one is the training facility for the Dallas Stars and the other for the Texas Tornado Junior Hockey League Champions. In addition, there is the Dr Pepper/Seven Up Ballpark, which was voted "best new ballpark" in 2003 and can accommodate 10,600 fans. The ballpark is home to the Frisco RoughRiders Double-A baseball team, an affiliate of the Texas Rangers. Frisco will also draw fans of championship cyclist racing. The Superdome, located at the Collin County Community College Preston Ridge Campus, is a world-class bicycle racing track and one of the fastest low altitude outdoor tracks in the world. The 2,200-seat stadium features a 250-meter, 44-degree banking inclined track, and was named "best Velodrome in North America." The Superdrome hosts a Friday night weekly series, which is open to the public. Soccer anyone? The Frisco Soccer and Entertainment Center is a soccer lover's dream come true. This facility, which is a 117-acre complex, is the first of its kind in the world! It includes a world-class stadium adjacent to 17 lighted, regulation-sized, tournament-grade soccer fields and will host international soccer games, major concerts, high school football and other marquee events!

If golf is "your bag," you will love playing the city's three exceptional courses, which include the award-winning Tom Fazio course at the Weston Stonebriar Resort, the Trails of Frisco and the Plantation Golf Club.

A Little Culture?

International and "uniquely Texas" art abounds in Frisco, but one of the most magnificent displays you absolutely must see is the Texas Sculpture Garden in the Hall Office Park along Dallas Parkway. The largest private collection on public display, the Texas Sculpture Garden features more than 40 contemporary sculptures by renowned Texas artists. Self-guided tours begin at the entrance to Hall Office Park at Dallas and Gaylord Parkways. Stroll through the garden, which winds around the lake, from dawn to dusk. Another must see is Central Park, just north of Gaylord Parkway and in The Centre at Preston Ridge. Stroll through Central Park and see longhorns and cowboys in a unique historic setting, or visit the popular shopping center to view a stampede of life-size longhorn cattle, cowboys, horses and an authentic cattle drive chuck wagon. Both the Hall Office Park and Central Park are settings for fabulous, Texas-sized festivals during the year, including Frisco Freedom Fest on the 4th of July, and the Great Steak of Texas Festival in October.

A Shopping and Dining Pleasure!

It is yours in Frisco, and it is all in a very family-friendly environment. Historic downtown Frisco offers fantastic shopping in a charming, quaint setting with enough small shops and boutiques to keep you busy all day—maybe two. Many of the original buildings have been restored and renovated, weaving the history of the town into the wonderful shopping experience. You will find clothing, antiques, jewelry, quilting supplies, flowers and beautiful home décor all within a few pretty blocks. Stop in one of the cafés or coffee shops for a sweet treat to enjoy at the gazebo at the corner of Fourth and Main Streets. Don't dawdle too long though, because there is so much more shopping to enjoy!

Whether you need "fast" fare to fit in with your shopping schedule or can enjoy "fine" dining at leisure, you will love the many opportunities in Frisco. There are several destination restaurants, as well as many that show off the true charm of Frisco. From steak (of course) and seafood to "cowboy grub" and heavenly hometown cooking, you will find it all here.

Whether you choose to shop, dine or play in Frisco, we know you will enjoy its charming blend of old and new. The pioneer spirit of its citizens has enabled the town to prosper into a true "destination" for visitors to the Dallas/Fort Worth Metroplex.

ALLEN

This growing and very prosperous city welcomes visitors with exciting opportunities and activities for all ages. Whether you have come to shop, golf or enjoy one of the many outdoor or indoor recreational activities, you will be pleasantly surprised by this community's offerings. It's a small city with big city opportunities.

European immigrants came by way of the Texas Road and the Central National Road during the early 1840s to take advantage of the advertised "free land," but it wasn't until 1872, when the Houston and Texas Central Railroad was constructed through Allen, that the township was actually laid out. With the railroad, Allen began to prosper. However, it was later devastated by fire in 1915, and by the time it was incorporated in 1953, it had a population of only about 400. Like the rail before it, US Hwy. 75 was constructed through Allen in 1960, leading the way for new businesses, jobs and incredible growth. This growth has continued as the result of much hard work. The effective leadership and determination of businessmen and women have made Allen a special place to live, work and play.

Art in Allen

You'll find an abundance of art in Allen, with four established community organizations bringing guest musicians, artists and authors throughout the year. The Allen Arts Alliance sponsors outdoor concerts and cultural activities such as Summer Sounds. The Allen Arts Alliance is the city's leading art organization, its mission is to promote, nurture and celebrate the world of art in Allen, Texas. The Friends of the Allen Public Library sponsor the highly acclaimed "Bach to Books" series, a venue of art programs that range from literary speakers to musical performances. The Allen Philharmonic Symphony was established in 1997, and now performs to sell-out crowds each weekend. And, the Heritage Allen Guild, which is dedicated to the preservation of the memory and spirit of the early settlers of Collin Country, maintains many historical properties throughout the area.

Outside Everyone!

Allen features the only still-standing stone dam in Texas that was at one time used for railroads. It is located along Cottonwood Creek, north of Exchange Pkwy. The site also contains the original foundation for the water tower. This area was designated as a State Archeological Landmark in 2001.

Allen has one of the last remaining native forests in North Texas. With it's beautiful winding trails that lie underneath gorgeous tree canopies; it is located along Rowlett Creek, west of Alma Dr.

Grab your swimming trunks, your fishing pole or your golf clubs! There are plenty of wonderful recreational opportunities in Allen. Nearby Lake Lavon is a 21,000-acre lake with 120 miles of shoreline, many parks and campsites. Anglers can cast for catfish, blue gill, perch, crappie, bass, white bass and more! Campers will appreciate the electric/water hookups, tent sites, boat ramps, fishing docks and rental services. Here, there is year-round water activity, which is always open to the public.

Allen's Chase Oaks Golf Club is a 27-hole golf course that features two individual courses: the Blackjack 18-hole course and the Sawtooth 9-hole course. Designed by architects Robert von Hagge and Bruce Devlin and constructed in 1986, the golf courses feature Tiff Eagle Bermuda Greens, tiff fairways, creeks, lakes, hills, and lots of trees. In 1991, the Blackjack course was named the Best Public Course in Texas by the *Dallas Morning News*. The course is also annually ranked in the Top 10 North Texas Courses by PGA members.

The entire family will love a day at Celebration Park with one of the largest handicap-accessible playgrounds in Texas, complete with a water spray ground, picnic facilities and a walking trail. Another popular place for outdoor fun hosted inside is the Don Rodenbaugh Natatorium, which features a large leisure pool with water play equipment, a flume slide, and lazy river. Another area in the facility features a large rock-climbing wall.

The Reason You're Here!

Allen's retail community is booming, so there are more and more wonderful shops and boutiques opening each year. The impressive Allen Premium Outlets opened in 2000 with more than 50 designer and name-brand stores, and this shopping haven has recently added another 12,000 square feet of retail space. You will also find a great number of specialty stores, gift boutiques and wonderful restaurants. Try them all!

For additional information about Plano, contact the Plano Convention and Visitors Bureau at 972-422-0296, 800-81-PLANO or visit online www.planocvb.com. Or, contact the Plano Chamber of Commerce at 972-424-7547 or visit www.planochamber.org online.

For more information about Frisco, contact the Frisco Chamber of Commerce at 972-355-9522, or visit www.friscochamber.com online. Or, contact the Frisco Convention and Visitors Bureau at 877-GOFRISCO or visit www.visitfrisco.com online.

For additional information about Allen, contact the Allen Chamber of Commerce at 972-727-5585, or visit www.allenchamber.com online.

Plano
Fairs Festivals & Fun

January
    Martin Luther King, Jr. Parade
       and Celebration
    Very Special Arts Festival

February
    Daddy's Little Sweetheart
       Dance
    Ms. Senior Plano Pageant
    Teen Mystery Night
    World of Cruises and Sun
       Destinations Showcase

March
    Country at Heart Craft Show
    House and Garden Show
    Plano Book Festival

April
    Blackland Prairie Festival
    Eggs Over Easy Easter Egg
       Hunt
    Great American Clean Up and
       Earth Fest
    It's a Natural

May
    Wildflower Run

June
    Juneteenth Celebration
    NPC Lone Star Bodybuilding
       and Fitness/Figure Classic
    Picnic in the Park

July
    July 4th Parade and
       Celebration

September
    Hot Air Balloon Festival
    Parrothead Phestival

October
    Fall Masquerade – Mother and
       Son Dance

November
    Christmas Crafts Fair

December
    Christmas Parade
    Dickens In Historic
       Downtown Plano

April
   Frisco RoughRiders Baseball

May
   FC Dallas Soccer

July
   Freedom Fest

September
   John Weinberg Golf Tournament
   Story Telling Festival
   Texas Tornado Hockey

October
   The Great Steak of Texas Festival

December
   Frisco Historic Tour of Homes
   Merry Main Street   Festival
   Santa Skate

Allen
Fairs Festivals & Fun

March
  Arbor Day

April
  Easter Egg Hunt

May
  All American Fishing Derby
  Summer Concert Series

June
  Summer Concert Series
  Allen USA Celebration

October
  Chocolate Orgy
  Harvest Festival

November
  St. Jude Craft Fair

December
  Holiday Craft Fair
  Holiday Tree Lighting Ceremony
  Library Gift Fair
  Rudolph Run

Cobwebs Antiques

When asked about a favorite place to "antique" in historic downtown Plano, locals could not say enough about Cobwebs Antiques, 1400 Avenue J (just one block from the DART rail station). Entering its 20th year, Cobwebs Antiques features quality antiques and collectibles from country to Victorian, with selections offered by 24 very knowledgeable dealers. Under the new management of Judy Rucker and Dr. Joseph Parker, Cobwebs Antiques continues a long established reputation for consistent quality. They are onsite daily to ensure excellence in both merchandise availability and customer service. Browse the beautiful vignettes, and then enjoy a delicious lunch at the French Hen Tea Room inside the mall. What a delightful way to spend the day! Cobwebs Antiques is open Monday-Saturday 10 am-5 pm, Sunday 1-5 pm. Lunch is served Tuesday-Saturday 11 am-2:30 pm. Call 972-423-8697.

Nature's Finest Art

When Susan Steblein discovered that her last name meant "little twig" in German, it all made perfect sense, because her passion has always been nature and the arts. Susan creates jewelry from very rare stones like Peruvian Opals, Druzies, Azurite and Baltic Amber, and has one of the largest collections of semiprecious jewelry in the Metroplex. You'll find rare stone jewelry, beautiful Salt Lamps, fossils, copper and wood art, as well as original paintings from some of the most talented artisans in the country. With more than 20 artists represented, there is always a collection of unique finds from California to New York. Her beautiful gallery, Nature's Finest Art, is located at 1016 E. 15th St., nestled in Plano's charming historic Main Street district and is open Monday 11 am - 5 pm and Tuesday-Saturday 10 am - 6 pm. For more information and extended holiday hours, call 972-898-7324. *(Color photo featured in front section of book.)*

Ask any child in Frisco about their favorite "party place" and they will shout; "Love You More." This amazing paint-your-own ceramics store is located at 6943 Main St. in Old Town Frisco. As you step into this 1920s building, you will enjoy the nostalgic atmosphere as you view the exposed brick walls and the ornate tin ceiling. Owners Effie and Tony Kenley stock hundreds of ceramic bisque pieces so young and old can come by anytime, grab a paintbrush, and have fun! If you are new to ceramics, or just want to learn a new technique, Effie and Tony offer several painting classes. There is also a private party room and "Story Time" every Wednesday morning. Open Monday-Saturday 10 am - 7 pm. For additional information or reservations, call 972-712-3700 or visit www.loveyoumoreceramics.com.

Bridal & Weddings

StarDust Celebrations

From the moment he gets down on one knee to "pop the question," the excitement begins. Whether you choose a date a year from that moment or plan something within the next month, there are thousands of decisions to make about the most special day in your lives together. It's lots of fun, but sometimes it can be very stressful, and that's where Jenny Cline and Marsha French come in. These charming, energetic, bride-and-groom-loving ladies can help you turn your wedding day into a celebration to be cherished forever. Let them do all of the work!

StarDust Celebrations, 2108 Dallas Pkwy. #228 in Plano, is a full-service wedding planning and wedding coordination service that includes 14 associates and a variety of part-time specialists. You can trust them completely with every decision. They have provided consulting services for weddings of all types, including church and home, large military, interfaith and destination weddings. They direct the rehearsal, and on the wedding day, coordinate the entire ceremony and reception. Throughout the planning process, Jenny and Marsha can recommend vendors, including: florists, photographers, bakeries, hair stylists and musicians, so that you'll have confidence in your choices.

When it comes time to choose the most important detail of the entire wedding, "the dress," you'll find an outstanding selection of beautiful gowns created by StarDust Designers here at the Plano Bridal Gown Salon, or at the second location, Lulu's Bridal Boutique, 2728 Routh St. in Dallas. Open Monday, Tuesday and Friday 10 am-6 pm, Wednesday-Thursday until 7 pm and Saturday until 5 pm. For information on consultation services, call 972-781-1619 or visit www.stardustcelebrations.com.

Children's

When you step into be-dazzled!, you'll find everything you'll need to decorate your child's bedroom or nursery, from traditional to exotic…from rustic to chic. This boutique features custom bedding and cribs, hand-painted and personalized gifts, furniture and accessories, and even hard-to-find items like camp trunks in non-traditional colors. With three talented artists on staff, who can personalize or customize almost any item in the store, you can turn your child's bedroom into a beautiful haven that will change and grow with your child.

According to owner Deb Hoffman, "Design is limited only to the imagination." And, there's plenty of imagination here! Located at 5760 Legacy Dr. in Plano, hours are Monday-Wednesday, Saturday 10 am - 6 pm and Thursday-Friday 10 am - 8 pm. For more information, call 972-378-3211 or go to www.bedazzledplano.com online.

Gourmet, Specialty Foods & Restaurants

Who says dieting has to be boring and unflavorful? Anyone who has tried the very popular Dr. Atkins Diet and other low-carb diets knows that after a few months of the same foods, you begin to crave variety—especially something sweet! Laura Strain had such great success with the Atkins program, that she decided to open a store that would cater to the public's demand for great-tasting, low-carb products.

Delicious-n-Fit, 4757 W. Park Blvd. #113 in Plano, has the largest selection of low-carb and sugar-free items in the entire Dallas metroplex area. You'll find all of the Atkins products, plus many delicious independent brands. Laura and her staff are very friendly and very knowledgeable about all of the products. Delicious-n-Fit is open Monday-Saturday 9 am-8 pm and Sunday noon-6 pm. Visit www.Delicious-n-Fit.com online or call 972-599-1018.

Be sure and check out Gloria's Restaurant of Frisco at 8600 Gaylord Pkwy. #5. See page 58 for full details.

Pomegranates
The Party Place

If you like to have fun, then Pomegranates—The Party Place —is for you! You'll find all-occasion gifts, unique greeting cards, fun party accessories, interesting ceramics and even gag-gifts. You'll also find a wonderful selection of long-lasting candles from the Tyler Candle Company, as well as specialty stationery and paper for newsletters. Pomegranates also offers custom printing and wedding invitations.

For more than 20 years, owner and operator Suzan Nix has offered reasonably-priced accessories and has created a fun, enjoyable shopping experience at Pomegranates! She enjoys sharing fun so much that she has two locations—the Plano store located at 4709 Parker Rd., #490 (call 972-867-6899) and the Dallas store located in Preston Center at 8411 Preston Rd., #102, (call 214-696-4550). Plan to stop by either store Monday-Friday from 10 am-6 pm and Saturday 10 am-5 pm.

T & T Hobby

Ladies, promise your guy a trip to T & T Hobby Shop, 3420 Ave. K, #154, and he might not mind tagging along on your "Day Out" in Plano. It's a great place to shop for your "boys" who still like their "toys!" You'll find the largest selection of battery- and-fuel-powered remote controlled cars in the DFW area, as well as aftermarket parts for the cars. They also stock battery-powered remote controlled model airplanes. Try to plan your visit on the first or third Sundays, 10 am-6 pm, to see the touring car races in the parking lot. Great fun! T & T Hobby is open Monday-Friday 11 am-6 pm and Saturday 10 am-6 pm. Call 972-633-2470.

TWO BROTHERS CIGARS

While ladies love shopping the unique boutiques and tearooms of Plano, guys don't mind at all being left behind here! Two Brothers Cigars, 1424 Ave. K, is a full-service tobacco shop offering cigar aficionados a wonderful selection of fine cigars from around the world. You'll also find pipes, lighters, humidors and a special blend of tobaccos. Guys aren't the only ones "lighting up" these days. Ladies love the "laid-back atmosphere" where they can also share a cup of coffee, watch television, and, of course, enjoy one of 120 brands of imported cigars. The two brothers, Greg and Rick Baldelli, invite you to visit their store Monday-Thursday 10 am - 6 pm, Friday-Saturday until 8 pm, or shop at www.twobrotherscigars.com. Call 972-424-7272.

Bacchus
F L O O R S

The Bacchus name is one that has been around for several generations in Frisco. In fact, Harold Bacchus, the founder of Bacchus Floors, was once the town's mayor. This family-owned- and-operated business, located at 6699 Main St., offers

the finest selections in carpet, hardwood flooring, ceramic tile and laminate. Their professional staff can assist with selection and schedule installation. The showroom is open Monday through Friday 8 am - 6 pm, Saturday 9 am - 5 pm and Sunday noon-4 pm. Call 972-335-1179 or visit www.bacchusfloors.com online.

Quilts, Needlework & Stitchery

Carriage House Quilt Shoppe

A "must" for any quilting enthusiast, The Carriage House Quilt Shoppe, 3000 Custer Rd., #170 in Plano, has been treating quilters to a remarkable selection of fabrics and supplies for more than 12 years. Owner Roxanne Rentzel carries yarn-dyed flannels, reproductions from the Civil War era, Aunt Grace, Thimbleberries, and a large selection of patriotic and western fabrics. There are packaged kits for almost every quilt in the store—beautiful, colorful creations that are sure to become treasured heirlooms. You'll find every notion known to quilters, as well as patterns—including their own line called CHQS—and many helpful books. The shop is open Monday 10 am - 8 pm, Tuesday-Friday until 6 pm and Saturday until 5 pm. Visit www.carriagehousequilts.com online or call 972-758-9916.

Woolie Ewe customers come from all walks of life—and they will travel across the country to shop here—to stock up on wonderful hand-dyed yarns, needlework and instructional books. Located at 1301 Custer Rd. #328 in Plano, The Woolie Ewe is a "feel-good" store filled with laughter and fun! Owner Sue Tuley and daughter Jill Brown offer instructional classes and friendly advice to their customers and friends, and it looks as though a third generation (granddaughters) may join the knitting ranks! They carry most major brands of yarn and needlework supplies, including Noro, Sirdar, Reynolds, Debbie Bliss and many more, as well as notions for knit, crochet and needlepoint projects. Open Monday-Friday 10 am-6 pm and Saturday until 4:30 pm. Call 972-424-3163 or visit www.wooliewe.com online. *(Color photo featured in front section of book.)*

Salon at Eaton Court

a full service Salon and Day Spa

Named by *D Magazine* as one of the "Top Salons and Spas" in the Dallas Metroplex, as well as the "Best of the Best" in 2004, Salon at Eaton Court will turn your next salon appointment into an extraordinary experience like no other. This beautifully restored Victorian cottage (expanded to 4,500 square feet) has been carefully designed to provide clients with a peaceful environment that is everything a salon and spa should be—a relaxing escape. Owner Kathleen Eaton, a finalist for the Collin County 2004 "Entrepreneur of the Year," has left no stone unturned in the meticulous attention to detail, from the hand-scraped hardwood floors, custom cabinetry, lush landscaping, picture-perfect front porch and stained glass windows to the unbelievably comfortable shiatsu massage shampoo chairs and bowls imported from Italy. Whether you're there for an hour or a day, you'll leave refreshed and renewed.

In addition to the designer haircuts and color, master stylists provide Balayage—a unique and personalized European method of highlighting hair. Salon at Eaton Court features exclusive products such as Kerastase Hair Treatments and custom-blended mineral cosmetics. And, under the direction of a medical director, Salon at Eaton Court offers the latest in skin resurfacing including personalized facials with medical and enzyme peels, waxing, permanent make-up, massage, body wraps, scrubs and natural nail manicures. Do you love pedicures? Well, the spa pedicures here have been rated by *D Magazine* as the best in Dallas, and have been described as "a spiritual experience that takes you to a place you've never been before."

Eaton Court's upper level is being designed to house a private luxury suite—the perfect destination for bridal parties, business meetings "spa style," small groups and the special client in search of total privacy and anonymity with special pampering that takes them to another time and place.

Salon at Eaton Court is conveniently located in Allen at 202 S. Austin St. (northwest corner of McDermott Dr. & Austin St.) and is open Tuesday-Thursday 9 am - 8 pm, Friday 9 am - 5 pm and Saturday 8 am - 6 pm. Visit www.eatoncourt.com online for prices, tour of the salon and spa, map/directions, packages and descriptions of services. Please call 972-727-2333 for appointments. Come and experience luxury at its finest! *(Color photo featured in front section of book.)*

FACE & BODY SPAS Be sure and check out Face & Body Spas of Frisco at 1549 Legacy Dr. See page 65 for full details.

Discover Rockwall
Garland/Richardson

ROCKWALL

There is a great place right in "the heart of North Texas" with enough history, mystery, culture, outdoor play and wonderful shopping to satisfy even the hard-to-please. Rockwall only minutes from Dallas, is an ideal setting for young families who want a slow, comfortable way of life, yet desire close proximity to big city adventure. It is located on the eastern shore of Lake Ray Hubbard, which opened as a water reservoir in 1968, and became a focal point for the community. Whether you are visiting Rockwall to investigate its mysterious namesake, enjoying a day of golf on one its challenging courses, or just "Shopping The Rock," you are in for an amazing adventure.

The Mysterious "Rock Wall"

When the earliest settlers found their way to Rockwall during the 1850s, there were three newcomers who were instrumental in naming this beautiful town—Mr. T. U. Wade, Mr. B. F. Boydston, and Mr. Stevenson. They had arrived to establish a "farming community," and began to investigate the land. History books tell us that the Mr. Wade began digging a well on the east side of the Trinity River valley and hit a "rock wall." The three pioneers had been arguing until this time about naming the town after themselves. With their fascinating discovery, they put their differences aside, and decided on "Rockwall." At that time, even with parts of the wall visible in places that stood two to three feet tall, the early settlers had no idea the scope of their early discovery.

Throughout the history of Rockwall, much excavation has revealed a mysterious underground stone formation that appears to circle the town. Many documented accounts by early residents describe cubicles or stone rooms, which you could walk through. Others tell of excavations of parts of the wall that go straight down as many as 40 feet and resemble a "buttress" used to support high standing structures. Some parts of the wall have previously been open to visitors during years, but are closed now because of dangerous structural conditions. A 1949 excavation produced four large stones (each weighing 2 tons) with inscriptions that appear to be pictographs.

The mysterious "rock wall" continues to baffle scientists and geologists today. Discovering the precise process that created this phenomenon, and trying to discover its beginning and original purpose, will keep scientists busy for many years, and keep visitors flocking to Rockwall. Stop by the Rockwall County Historical Foundation Museum for a visit through the smallest county in Texas or call 972-722-1507 to find out more.

Rock Steady Future

One sign that you will see almost everywhere in Rockwall today is, "Under Construction." The town is booming with new residential and commercial developments underway in every direction. The Rockwall Technology Park draws Fortune 1000 and Fortune 500 companies to Rockwall, which then boosts the city's economy. The future of Rockwall is what you might call, "Rock Steady."

One of the city's most special attractions is, of course, the beautiful Lake Ray Hubbard. The lake offers abundant opportunities for recreation, including 14 miles of prime inland sailing. You'll find seven marinas and two yacht clubs offering waterskiing, boating, swimming and fishing. And, there are two championship golf courses. Buffalo Creek is rated one of America's top courses, receiving many accolades from golf magazines. Another wonderful course, The Shores, offers the amazing ambience of the lake along some of its 18 holes. It's truly a challenging golfing adventure.

Ladies on their day out in Rockwall will be delighted to find that for a small city, there is quite a lot to cover. Shopping centers and shopping villages dot the area, featuring everything from stained glass and stamping supplies to antiques and fine art. Look for the quaint yellow cottages in the heart of Rockwall called Goliad Place, and enjoy an entire day of fun, food and full spa service. And, whether you want to grab a quick bite from a fast food eatery, or enjoy a leisurely lunch at a charming tearoom, you'll find it here in Rockwall. Your experience will be a delightful escape from big city fuss. Rockwall, Texas, can be described as "just minutes away, yet worlds apart."*(Color photo featured in front section of book.)*

GARLAND

The city leaders of Garland tout it as, "A Progressive Environment with Excellent Opportunities" and "the Home Sweet Home Community of the Metroplex." There are more than 220,600 people living in Garland, making it the 10th largest city in Texas, and the 82nd largest in the United States. The DART Light Rail Line offers convenient travel, and the Dallas/Fort Worth International Airport is only 30 minutes away. Even though the city is just 15 miles northeast of downtown Dallas, it retains its hometown atmosphere. And, it has one of the highest percentages of married couples and home ownership in the area.

Garland History

Long before Texas attained statehood in 1846, Garland was known as part of the "Peters colony," which was a venture by W.S. Peters. In 1850, settlers made their way by wagon to this area, through acres of wildflowers, bottomlands and even bands of Indians! A store was built in 1874 and later a corn mill, which was built on the northwest bank of "Duck Creek." In fact, that's what the first community was called. By 1867, two cotton gins had been built. And, a decade later, a post office was established. As happened many times in the early west, a community's growth depended on the proximity of the railroad. In 1886, the Santa Fe Railroad built its line and depot almost a mile away from Duck Creek, and the village that sprouted up there was called Embree, after the prominent physician Dr. K.H. Embree. A battle ensued between the communities of Embree, Duck Creek, and a new Duck Creek until 1887. That's when the government named the location, which combined the communities, "Garland" in honor of then Attorney General A.H. Garland.

Just east of Garland's City Hall, you will find what is referred to as the historic "Heritage Park." It contains the Santa Fe Railroad Depot, a Santa Fe railroad passenger car, the Lyles House and the Pace House. A visit to Heritage Park should be a priority when visiting Garland because it is such a perfect slice of the city's early history. The depot is now known as the Garland Landmark Museum. It houses the museum that contains memorabilia from Garland's early days, early settler's artifacts, old newspapers, farm implements and quilts.

The Pace House is a beautifully restored Victorian home that was built in 1895 by John Pace. It was originally constructed as the main house for the Pace's surrounding farm, and was moved to its current location in Heritage Park in 1985. The one-story asymmetrical architecture is described as an excellent example of the vernacular Texas Victorian farmhouse. The gables and dormers were decorated with imbricated shingles, and the porches have wooden-turned columns and a "spindle frieze gingerbread" that encircles the upper portion of the porch. The Pace House has a wonderful ambiance, which lends itself perfectly to parties, receptions and special events. And, it can accommodate up to 100 people. This Victorian house is an integral part of Garland's history, and continues to create a story of its own as it hosts countless events throughout the year.

Recreation and Culture

Downtown Garland offers visitors a variety of facilities for wonderful social activities, including theaters, museums, wonderful shopping opportunities and restaurants. We spent quite a few wonderful hours browsing McGillicuddy's Antiques in the downtown district, and then settled down at the tearoom for a wonderful lunch. The town is also home to some of the most famous fried chicken in the state. Babe's Chicken Dinner House has been praised in *Southern Living* as one of the all time favorite places for fried chicken. If your family loves the great outdoors, the Garland Parks and Recreation Department provides a broad range of programs through its park system that includes more than 25,000 acres of parkland. In fact, there are 69 city parks, 37 tennis courts and three city swimming pools. The Firewheel Golf Park's 63 championship holes will challenge the most experienced golfer, and Lake Ray Hubbard is the perfect playground for camping, boating, fishing and swimming.

The Patty Granville Arts Center at Austin and Fifth Streets is the center stage for wonderful theater productions, as well as the location for functions put on by private groups and civic organizations. The Garland Cultural Arts Commission was established in 1986 to serve as a liaison for the city, and it's been a major contributor to the advancement of the arts in Garland. It now has five major affiliate organizations. The Garland Landmark Museum Society is located one block from City Hall in the restored 1901 Santa Fe Railroad Depot. It contains artifacts dating back to the 1850s. The Garland Civic Theatre, founded in 1968, is the oldest community theater group in Dallas County. The Garland Summer Musicals, founded in 1983, produces highly acclaimed Broadway musicals. The Garland Symphony Orchestra, founded in 1978, offers six concerts annually. And, the Garland Country Music Association sponsors the "Big G" Jamboree with western and gospel bluegrass groups. The city is also very proud that the historic Plaza Theatre has once again opened in Garland. The newly-renovated theatre has a spacious auditorium, a stage for productions and meetings, and a beautiful art deco lobby perfect for special receptions.

Star Spangled Fourth

Garland's signature event is its award-winning Independence Day celebration, Start Spangled Fourth. This multi-day festival features three stages of live entertainment, a huge midway, a special fun-filled entertainment zone just for kids, a delicious food court, unique crafters, a multicultural arts exhibit and much more. Event details are available at www.starspangledfourth.com.

Happy Holidays!

If you are lucky enough to visit Garland during the holidays, you will be delighted with Christmas on the Square, the holiday festival that takes place in the historic downtown area. The entire place is decorated with thousands of sparkling lights. Plus, the festive Parade of Lights provides a beautiful entrance into the Christmas holidays.

RICHARDSON

The affluent suburban city of Richardson used to be described as a "little bedroom community of the 50s and 60s." Today, Richardson is a vibrant community with a huge emphasis on the cultural and performing arts, and is at the heart of a significant employment center called the Telecom Corridor®. This city of 100,000 works hard to maintain a wonderful quality of life for its citizens, as well as provide plenty of recreational opportunities for its visitors.

Richardson: Then and Now

When settlers from Tennessee and Kentucky began arriving in this part of Texas during the 1840s, the Comanche and Caddo Indian tribes inhabited this land. Many of the earliest families put their wagons in a circle around an area that was later named Breckinridge, in honor of the U.S. Vice President. The railroad, however, bypassed Breckinridge for a site just to the northwest, and that little area instantly became the new center for activity. Richardson was named for the railroad contractor E.H. Richardson, and was chartered in 1873.

Fast-forward to 1954; that's when the Central Expressway opened in Dallas and the agricultural city of the past became a city of residential homes and shopping centers. It has been non-stop growth ever since, with the electronic age ushering in an entire new image for Richardson.

Richardson is home to the Telecom Corridor®, a defined geographic area encompassing one of the highest concentrations of leading-edge communications and technology-based companies in the world. The origins of the Telecom date back to the 1950s when Texas Instruments located its corporate headquarters at the Intersection of US 75 and LBJ Freeway. The following years saw companies such as Alcatel, MCI, Nortel, Fujitsu and Ericsson locate here, making the Telecom Corridor® a world-class center for telecommunications. If you were to look at the Telecom Corridor® from above, you would see that it is mapped out in the shape of the letter "T." The 5-mile leg of the "T" lies along North Central Expressway, and the crosshatch of the "T" lies along the south side of President George Bush Highway.

Things to Do and See

The Charles W. Eisemann Center for the Performing Arts and Corporate Presentations, which includes a 1500-seat performance hall, is the perfect venue for performing arts groups, corporate meetings and special events. The Eisemann Center also presents professional musical, dance, comedy and theatrical events. Other favorite attractions are the Owens Spring Creek Farm, with its museum dating back to 1928 and Miss Belle's Place, Richardson's first schoolhouse circa 1887. The Richardson park system enables visitors to enjoy a natural setting or provide a diverse set of recreational activities, which provides fun for the whole family.

Wonderful Wildflower

If you happen to be in Richardson during the month of May, you just might happen onto one of the city's most exciting and extraordinary events. Wildflower! Festival features the best in unique local, regional and national entertainment on five stages. You'll hear jazz, blues, rock, country, folk, R&B, and swing. The entire family will delight in the spectacular Arts and Crafts Marketplace, the impromptu performances of acrobats and musicians, and nightly concerts in the Hill Hall. Wildflower! Festival was recently named "Best of the Fests" by *D Magazine*, so don't miss a minute.

For more information about Rockwall, contact the Rockwall Area Chamber of Commerce at 972-771-5733, or visit www.rockwallchamber.org online. Or, contact the City of Rockwall at 972-771-770 or visit www.rockwall.com online.

For additional information about Garland, contact the Garland Chamber of Commerce at 972-272-7551, or visit www.garlandchamber.com online. Or, contact the Garland Convention and Visitors Bureau at 972-205-2749 or visit www.ci.garland.tx.us online.

For additional information about Richardson, contact the Richardson Chamber of Commerce at 972-234-4141, or visit www.telecomcorridor.com online. Or, contact the Richardson Convention & Visitors Bureau at 888-690-7287, 972-744-4037 or visit www.richardsontexas.org online.

Garland Fairs Festivals & Fun

January
   Martin Luther King, Jr. Parade

April
   Garland Area American Cancer Society Relay for Life
   Watson Technology Center Fun Run/Walk

May
   Angels in Blue 5K Run
   Fishing Derby

July
   Star Spangled Fourth

September
   16 de Septiembre Fiesta
   Jaycees Labor Day Parade

November
   Veterans Day Tribute

December
   Christmas on the Square

Rockwall Fairs Festivals & Fun

February
Daddy/Daughter Dance

April
Easter Egg Hunt
Founder's Day Festival
Rotary and Chamber Taste of
    Rockwall & Business Expo
Women's League Charity Ball

May
Arts and Crafts Fair
Concerts by the Lake (May-
    July)
Mother/Son Hoedown

June
Rockwall Open Golf
    Tournament

July
Fireworks & Music Show
Movies in the Park

August
Movies in the Park

September
Arts and Crafts Fair

October
Fishing Derby
Friends of the Library
    Pumpkin Patch
Halloween Carnival and
    Extravaganza
Jazz in the Park

December
Christmas Parade
Christmas Tree Lighting and
    Laser Light Show
Lunch with Santa

Richardson
Fairs Festivals & Fun

May
Wildflower Arts and Music Festival
Cottonwood Art Festival

July
Family 4th Celebration

September
Great Fountain Plaza Festival

October
Cottonwood Arts Festival
Huffhines Art Trails

December
Santa's Village

Antiques

It has been called, "A Feast For the Eyes," "A Festival of Flavors," and "A Taste of Europe on Rockwall's Square." The French Pear, 106 S. Goliad, is the culmination of a life-long dream for owner Kim Hoegger, who combined her talent in interior design, obsession with beautiful things, and love of people to create this European gift shop and café. You will find American and European antiques, beautifully upholstered sofas and chairs, French walnut inlaid tables, Lampe Bergere, as well as European and antique bed, bath and kitchen linens. Shop, and then cross the cobblestone patio to the adorable café for the most delicious homemade soups, quiches, sandwiches, salads and delectable desserts. The French Pear is an unforgettable treat! The store is open Monday-Saturday 9:30 am - 5:30 pm. Lunch is served in the café 11 am - 3 pm, and coffee, tea and dessert are featured 3 - 5 pm. The café is also open for breakfast on Saturday 9 - 11 am. Call 972-772-2995 or visit www.thefrenchpear.biz.

When Karen and Robert Scott learned that the old 1897 "Odd Fellows" building at 113 N. 6th St. in Garland was for sale, they knew that it would be the perfect place for their antiques and treasures. They worked three long months getting it ready to open as McGillicuddy's Antiques. Karen has been in the antique business for more than 20 years, and specializes in unique American antiques. She likes to research every piece she buys—learning the history and unique features of the antique—so she can pass the information on to the new owner. You will find wonderful glassware, pottery, jewelry and quilts, and the prices are very reasonable. Customers tell us that McGillicuddy's Antiques is the best-kept secret in the Dallas Metroplex! It is open Tuesday, Thursday, Friday and Saturday 11 am-5 pm and Wednesday until 2 pm. For more information, call 972-494-7448.

The Avenue
Classic Antiques & Interiors

As you stroll into The Avenue, you become enveloped by the warmth, elegance and grace of classical architecture, stonewalls, 18th and 19th century furnishings, and distinguished interiors. Ladies will find everything they need in "The Boutique" featuring Brighton, Karen Kane Casuals, Bentleya, Yves Delorme, Nicole Miller, French parfums and much more! The Avenue, 102 E. Rusk in Rockwall, is open Monday through Saturday 9:30 am-6 pm. For more information, call owner Lina Thompson at 972-722-5567.

Artists & Art Galleries

STAINED GLASS
C R E A T I O N S

Looking for unique stained glass? Rebecca Hill's "Stained Glass Creations" makes everything from lampshades to decorative cabinet doors and windows. Rebecca also offers stained glass classes and repairs. Her studio is located in Rockwall, but she works strictly by appointment. Rebecca even works from photos, and she can incorporate unique elements such as lace, mineral samples or shells into the glass design. For an appointment, call 972-771-4123.

Attractions & Entertainment

Plaza Theatre

A focal point and Garland landmark since the 1940s, the historic Plaza Theatre, located at 521 W. State St., has now reached its finest hour. From the spectacular chandelier and spacious domed lobby, to the luxurious velvet seating and motorized waterfall curtain, the Plaza has been lovingly refurbished in the art deco style. The Plaza was one of three theatres owned by H.R. and Jennie Bisby, and in its time, the Plaza was considered the most modern complex in the suburban Garland area. Its current façade was designed in 1950 by Dallas architect Jack Grogan, and the spiraling neon sign remains a beacon in the downtown historic square. The Plaza was donated to the City of Garland by Sherri and John Skelton II in 1991 in memory of the Bisbys, and renovated to its current exquisite state in 2001. With its state-of-the-art lighting and sound systems,

the 350 seat theatre is the perfect setting for the finest stage productions, concerts, business meetings, receptions and special events. The Plaza Theatre is available for events seven days a week. For scheduling information, call 972-205-2782 or visit www.garlandarts.com online.

The Granville Arts Center was renamed in 2003 in honor of Patty Granville, Director of the Performing Arts Center since its opening in 1982. More than 150,000 people visit the Granville Arts Center each year to attend hundreds of plays, seminars, receptions and concerts. The beautifully renovated Granville Arts Center provides two elegant proscenium theatres with seating for 200 or 720. The Main Auditorium—with plush seats, green carpet and warm wood walls—provides the perfect setting for musicals, symphony performances, ballets and concerts. The Small Theatre, with a dramatic décor of red carpet and seats, is an intimate setting for smaller productions. The Center also includes a magnificent Atrium, a 6,500 square foot ballroom encased in glass on two sides, open to a beautiful courtyard. These venues are available to civic, community or commercial organizations seven days a week and provide the community with rental facilities that rival any other in the Metroplex. The Granville Arts Center, located at 300 N. Fifth St. in Garland, is available for events seven days a week. For information call 972-205-2780, for box office reservations call 972-205-2790, or visit www.garlandarts.com online.

Because pineapples represent "welcome and hospitality," Lynn Davis chose them as her "signature" throughout L'Egantz, 206 E. Rusk St. in Rockwall. They signify the warmth and helpful attitude that permeates this remarkable home décor and gift shop. You'll find distinctive, elegant treasures for every room in your home. L'Egantz is open Tuesday-Thursday 10 am-6 pm and Friday-Saturday until 5 pm. For more information, visit www.legantz.com online or call 972-771-3600.

PRISSY'S

Family-owned-and-operated since 1985, Prissy's Hallmark, 447 E. I-30, has become a well-loved tradition in Rockwall. Owner Prissy Hein and long-time "store manager" Stevie—her 18-year-old Pomeranian—carry a large selection of Precious Moments and Willow Tree Angel collectibles, as well as cards and art by artist Jackson Hale, a former resident of Rockwall. Prissy's Hallmark is open Monday-Saturday 10 am-6:30 pm and Sunday noon-5 pm. For more information, call 972-722-3835.

Rockwall Flowers & Gifts, 102 S. Goliad St., has served the City of Rockwall as a florist for more than 60 years. For the last 16 years, it has been family-owned-and-operated by Jenny Murray, who along with her mother and daughter, have provided outstanding floral design. You'll find exquisite gifts for the home, extraordinary arrangements and beautiful flowers. Open Monday-Friday 9 am-5 pm and Saturday until noon. Call 972-771-6911, 800-876-2736 or visit www.rockwallflowers.com.

Hotels

RICHARDSON

Talk about a good location! The Hampton Inn, 1577 Gateway Blvd., is in the heart of Richardson's Telecom Corridor, with Nortel, Cisco Systems, MCI, SBC, Ericsson and more. Minutes away from dynamic downtown Dallas, the spacious rooms feature wireless high speed Internet, free local calls, coffee makers, iron and ironing boards. The Hampton Inn also has a complimentary hot deluxe breakfast and an outdoor pool. For reservations, call 800-HAMPTON, 972-234-5400 or visit www.hamptoninn.com.

The first clue that you are in for some of the best fried chicken in Texas is the usually large crowd waiting at the front door of Babe's Chicken Dinner House. The second, of course, is the unmistakable smell of crispy fried chicken and homemade biscuits. Babe's Chicken Dinner House, 1456 Beltline Rd. in Garland has been touted by *Southern Living Magazine* and fried chicken aficionados as one of the top choices in the state for finger-lick'n fried chicken. Owners Mary Beth and Paul Vinyard grew up on simple West Texas country food and wanted to duplicate those same delicious dishes in their restaurants. From the first bite of crispy fried chicken to the last scrumptious crumb of homemade pie, Babe's Chicken Dinner House certainly lives up to its reputation.

Of course, Babe's is known for much more than its wonderful food. It's also known for its kooky ad campaigns. Ever heard of the Mutkens? They are fictitious 7-foot-tall giant chickens who terrorize Texas, or at least they did until Paul put them in their place with the help of his R.A.V. (Roundup and Assault Vehicle). He is on duty night and day (when he's not cooking great chicken) destroying all Mutkens. His R.A.V. is a sight to behold. Actually, it's an old Harvester Fire Truck turned into a zebra-camouflaged war vehicle. It certainly puts the fear of God into the Mutkens! While the Mutkens usually feed on grain, rumor has it they've eaten goats, sheep, cats, dogs and even the occasional short person! So, beware! There might be a Mutken lurking around your backdoor. If so, give Paul a call.

Your choices at Babe's—fried chicken , chicken fried steak, fried chicken fingers, pot roast, fried catfish, hickory smoked chicken or spare ribs, with sides that will satisfy your Southern soul.

Heaping platters of piping hot entrees are followed by bowls of buttery mashed potatoes smothered in rich creamy gravy, sweet Grandma's corn, green beans, and soft, flaky homemade biscuits. Mary Beth says, "We make our biscuits one little-old pan at a time." And, to finish it off, be sure to save some room for a slice of one of their delicious homemade pies or banana pudding!

They sure do something right, because Babe's Chicken Dinner House has caught the attention of the Food Network, that featured Babe's in the segment "Classic Chicken."

The Vinyard family is quite famous throughout Texas for their fried chicken empire. Mary Beth and Paul, with the help of their children, own and operate Bubba's Cooks Country, and will soon open their fourth Babe's Chicken Dinner House (See pages 59 & 78). This is truly some of the best fried chicken in the South! Babe's is open Tuesday-Friday 11 am-2 pm for lunch and 5-9 pm for dinner, Saturday 11 am-9 pm and Sunday 11 am-3 pm. Call 972-496-1041. *(Color photo featured in front section of book.)*

During the day, light floods beautifully through two sides of The Atrium at the Granville Arts Center, and the view through the floor-to-ceiling windows is a magnificently landscaped courtyard. At night, this contemporary center takes on an entirely different atmosphere. Sparkling lights from the city shine through the glass, and ceiling lights can colorfully spotlight a beautiful centerpiece, a wedding cake or a dancing bride and groom. It's the perfect location for weddings, anniversaries, receptions and a wide variety of other social events. With seating for up to 500 people—non-profit and corporate groups find it perfect for banquets, fund-raisers, concerts or seminars. The Atrium at the Granville Arts Center, 300 N. Fifth St., is next to the DART Light Rail Station in Garland. Available for events seven days a week, call 972-205-3981 for more information or visit online at www.garlandarts.com. *(Color photo featured in front section of book.)*

Value

Be sure and check out Seconds & Surplus Building Materials of Richardson at 124 E. Arapaho. See page 47 for full details.

Discover Sherman

The town of Sherman was created by an act of the 1846 Texas Legislature, and designated as the County Seat for Grayson County. With the opening of the town's United States Post Office in 1847, Sherman began to see new settlers moving into the community, and it began to prosper as a merchandising center. The town was named for General Sidney Sherman, a hero of the Texas Revolution, who is credited with the famous battle cry, "Remember the Alamo!" General Sidney Sherman was born in Marlboro, Mass., in 1805. He was orphaned at age 16, and was an entrepreneur from that time on. In 1831, he formed a company to make bagging by machinery, and is believed to have been one of the first to make sheet lead. During the early days of the revolution, Sherman was so committed to the cause that he sold his cotton bagging plant and used the money to form and equip a company of volunteers in Kentucky. Sherman and his volunteers reached Texas the day before the delegate election for the Convention of 1836, and received the right to vote. It was on April 21, 1836, that Sherman commanded the left wing of the Texas army and opened the attack at the Battle of San Jacinto. Sherman and his family later settled in a one-room log house on a bluff below the San Jacinto battleground.

In the Beginning

During its earliest days as a small western frontier town in the 1850s, Sherman developed quite a bad reputation, earning the nickname of "Helldorado on the Cross Timbers." By 1860, the county had established an armed detachment of men to patrol the area in search of runaway slaves and abolitionists, and shortly after the war, outlaw bands led by Jesse James and William Quantrill roamed the area. The 1870s, at last, brought peace, prosperity and growth to Sherman, and a population of almost 6,000. Austin College was established in Sherman in 1876, and it's partly the reason for the city's more complimentary moniker, "The Athens of Texas."

Unfortunately, Sherman will always be haunted with the notoriety of being the scene of one of the South's major race riots. In 1930, a racially motivated mob stormed the courthouse and burned it to the ground and a period of rioting and violence erupted throughout the city. With the Great Depression fast on the heels of the fire, the growth of Sherman declined somewhat until 1941 when the federal government constructed a pilot training base called Perrin Army Air Field in Sherman. Additionally, the building of Denison Dam and Lake Texoma ushered in postwar growth, and then oil was discovered in the city during the 1950s.

Savor the Sights and Events

Sherman is known today as "The Gateway to Lake Texoma," and enjoys a substantial amount of tourism. Located on the Red River, with more than 600 miles of shoreline, Lake Texoma covers 89,000 acres, and is renowned throughout the United States for its world-class striped bass fishing and deepwater opportunities. Sherman continues to maintain a leadership role as an industrial center and retail hub, and has garnered a reputation as being a city of great opportunity for the arts, music and theater. The Sherman Symphony, part of Austin College's Community Series, presents various programs during the year, featuring world-renowned pianists, all-orchestral programs and choirs from area universities. If you enjoy outdoor concerts, you won't want to miss Hot Summer Nights every Thursday evening during the months of June and July. Sherman also boasts a wonderful Community Theater, and the beautifully restored Kidd-Key Auditorium, which is a marvelous performing arts venue for the entire county.

A Day Out on the Town

Visitors to Sherman will find a multitude of opportunities for great family fun and extraordinary shopping. Be sure to save time for a trip to the Grayson County Frontier Village Museum, which affords a walk back in time to the days when pioneers used hand tools to notch together logs for their cabins. The museum is filled with historical photographs and artifacts from the county's earliest days. The Red River Historical Museum on Pecan Street is another exciting way to view the history of Sherman and Grayson County.

Outdoor enthusiasts will love the 4-mile, self-guided tour through the Hagenman Natural Wildlife Refuge (NWR). The NWR offers birders wonderful sightings of birds in every season, from sparrows to scissor-tailed flycatchers. There are fascinating places for photography, hiking, boating, fishing and even some hunting.

Ahhh…shopping—we've saved the best for last! Sherman is a remarkable place to shop, and the best place to start may be the beautiful historical downtown square. You will find everything from antiques to apple pie, and just about everything in between. We loved Kelly Square. It was originally a group of four buildings, which were believed to have been built during the 1870s after the city's fire of 1875. A trunk salesman by the name of Leo Kelly purchased the four buildings around 1917 and placed a common brick façade around them. You can still see his name in concrete at the top of the building. Kelly Square has been renovated with a charming sense of yesteryear, and offers shoppers a delightful experience. Piano music sets the tone for lunch diners in two restaurants in the Square, while visitors browse through home accessory shops, clothing boutiques, jewelry and antique stores. In the following pages you will find even more great shops so read on!

For a town that started with a nickname like Helldorado, Sherman has grown into a beautiful community respected far and wide for its cultural and educational opportunities. We know that you will enjoy discovering the "Red River, White Stars, Blue Sky!" Being just one hour north of Dallas on Hwy. 75, Sherman is close enough to get there yet far enough to get away. The "Retroplex" of North Texas…enjoy all the comforts of the country with city sophistication.

For more information about Sherman, contact the Sherman Department of Tourism at 888-893-1188, 903-893-1184 or visit www.shermantx.org online.

Sherman Fairs Festivals & Fun

March
Texoma Exposition and Stockshow

April
Charity Ball
LakeFest Regatta
Red River Valley Birding and Nature Festival
Sherman Preservation League Tour of Homes

June
Hot Summer Nights

July
Hot Summer Nights
Jazz on July 3rd

September
Hispanic Heritage Festival
International Aerobatic Competition
Kelly Square Arts Fest
Sherman Arts Festival

October
Grayson County Fair

November
Grayson County Holiday Lights at Loy Lake Park
Kelly Square Holiday Open House

December
Altrusa Christmas Pilgrimage of Homes
Christmas Parade and Snowflake Festival
Community Series Christmas Pops

SQUARE

The historic 1870 "Kelly Square" in downtown Sherman seems to have escaped time, retaining a wonderful turn-of-the-century charm for all to enjoy. The four buildings that now compose Kelly Square were renovated with the addition of a common brick façade between 1916 and 1917, but the present restoration was completed in 1983. Owners Robert and Honey Minshew have captured the original integrity of the historic buildings with attention to details that make it a truly remarkable piece of history. It is filled with wonderful specialty shops— creating that perfect ambiance for "a lady's day out."

Honey Minshew's **"Gifts by Petite Fleur"** is a magnificent store filled with special gifts from Lady Primrose, Vera Bradley, Simon Pierce and Waterford. She also offers a bridal registry. Visit www.giftsbypetitefleur.com or call 903-892-4971.

Kelly's Restaurant and Catering serves lunch from 11 am- 2 pm and the piano music is played from noon-1 pm creating a delightful atmosphere for lunch with friends. 903-892-8409.

If you're a kid at heart, you'll love **Treasures, Toys & Gifts**, 903-893-4775, which features incredible items for children of all ages.

Garden Gate, 903-870-9894, showcases wonderful antiques, garden iron, wreaths, garlands, jewelry and fragrant candles.

For all of your floral and home décor needs, be sure to visit Shannon Scoggins at **Special Occasions**, 903-868-0999 or visit online at www.special-occasions-flowers.com.

Visit **Happenings**, 903-813-3311, for fine women's apparel and beautiful fashion accessories.

Kelly Square has ushered in a revitalization and growth to Sherman's downtown that has made it one of the most fascinating places to shop in the Dallas area. The Shops in the Square are open Monday through Friday 10 am-5:30 p.m. and Saturday 10 am- 5 pm.

Antiques

A Touch of Class Antique Mall

"Some of the best Antique Dealers in the Southwest!" is the slogan of A Touch of Class Antique Mall, and we're sure you'll agree. Located in Sherman's historic downtown square, the building is a Texas Historic Landmark and listed on The National Registry of Historic Places. A Touch of Class offers you more than 38,000 square feet of shopping, as well as a glimpse into the Grayson County's history. Owners Jeanette and Ivert Mayhugh have transformed the space into one of the most respected antique malls in the state. It was voted the "Best Antique Shop" by the *Herald Democrat* of Texoma and has also been featured in *Antique Travelers* magazine. Individual dealers fill the first two floors with more than 150 booths, offering fine furniture, quality glassware, vintage jewelry, Primitives, clocks, books, art and military memorabilia. The third floor is a museum dedicated to Grayson County, a real treat for locals and visitors. A Touch of Class also makes you feel right at home during the holidays, featuring wonderful Christmas shopping and elaborate decorations, earning it First Place for Best Outside Decorated Store in the area. And, near Valentine's Day, the mall hosts an Annual Mother-Daughter Tea. A Touch of Class, 118 W. Lamar St., is open Monday through Saturday 9:30 am-5:30 pm and Sunday 11 am-5 pm. For more information, call 903-891-9379.

Brenda's Antiques & Gifts

Brenda Ramey was at a crossroad in her life and decided to take a chance. After some soul searching, she summoned her courage and made a long time dream come true. She opened Brenda's Antiques & Gifts at 221 S. Travis in Sherman, and absolutely loves every minute of her new life. Many customers reminisce about the old days of the building when it was a grocery store. Today, it looks like something out of a design magazine. Brenda has worked magic with displays that include antique furniture and primitive décor, even thoughtful sayings painted on the walls. The staff is extremely helpful and friendly. This is a shop you must see! Brenda's Antiques & Gifts is open Tuesday-Saturday 10:30 am - 5 pm. Call 903-891-0400.

Artists, Art Galleries & Framing

Gallery Frames & Art Center

One thing that distinguishes Gallery Frames & Art Center from any other is the individual attention given to each customer's framing needs. Owner Greg Ashby will make sure that your artwork, photograph or memorabilia is framed exactly as ordered. Greg opened his first store in Sherman in 1987 and the present shop at 120 E. Mulberry, in 1999. He carries Gamblin Artist Oil Colors and DaVinci Artist Brushes, and he has the knowledge to answer all the questions you have about art. You will find a remarkable selection of artwork, including originals by Greg—who has won two local Art League awards and was featured in a one-man show at the local community theater. The gallery also features some of the finest artists in North Texas and Southern Oklahoma. The gallery is open Monday-Friday 9 am - 5 pm and Saturday until 1 pm. Call 903-892-3113.

Three Sisters Victorian Inn

When you step into the beautiful Victorian foyer you will feel as though you have truly stepped back in time. Three Sisters Victorian Inn, 506 N. Grand Ave., is a 100-year-old restored Victorian home, a resplendent reminder of Sherman's turn-of-the-20th-  century history. Owner Elta Rumpff has named the inn for her beautiful granddaughters Abigail, Amanda and Ashley, and the rooms bearing their names are filled with extraordinary antiques and furnishings. And, many of these beautiful antiques are for sale. The inn also features seven cast iron fireplaces and Elta's interesting collection of antique clocks. Breakfast is served in splendor each morning in the dining room, and a wrap around porch provides the perfect place to enjoy refreshing lemonade during the day. For information or reservations, visit www.threesistersvictorianinn.com online or call 903-868-4697.

Florists

Shannon and Neil Scoggins believe that "flowers speak when words fail," and are dedicated to presenting remarkable floral arrangements that will add beauty and romance to any "special occasion." Their enchanting flower shop at 115 S. Travis St. in Sherman is filled with unique containers filled with impeccable blossoms, bundles and bundles of fresh flowers, and unique and beautiful gifts. Their design talents range from the "Garden Style of Europe" to the "Sleek Design of New York." Words cannot describe the beauty and elegance of their work. The flowers speak for themselves. Special Occasions, located in one of the many shops inside the historic Kelly building in downtown Sherman, is open Monday-Friday 10 am - 5:30 pm and Saturday until 5 pm. To see samples of their extraordinary designs, be sure to visit www.special-occasions-flowers.com online or call 903-868-0999.

Gifts, Home Décor & Specialty Shops

Wow! If you want just a little reminder of your fabulous trip to Texas, we've found the perfect place to shop. T-Shirts N Texas, 324 N. Travis St. in Sherman, is a shop dedicated solely to the history, pride and humor of the Lone Star State. The selection of Texas gifts includes flags, clothing, books, artwork, license plates, mugs, wind chimes and, of course, wonderful Texas T-Shirts. Searching for that perfect gift? You're bound to find it here. Or, let the caring staff create a wonderful gift basket for that special someone filled with an assortment of wonderful made-in-Texas gourmet foods like salsas, hot sauce, spices and candy; a Texas cookbook; an apron; bumper stickers; framed art; and more! Open Monday-Saturday 10 am-5:30 pm. For a great look at the vast selection of wonderful Texas gifts, visit www.tshirtsntexas.com online or call 903-892-1072. Their slogan—"We're loud 'n proud 'bout the state of Texas and our Great Nation!"—really says it all. You're going to love this store—even if you weren't born in Texas.

MEMORY MUSIC
MUSIC MEMORABILIA

From *Blue Suede Shoes* and *Pretty Woman* to *Hotel California* and *Me and Bobby McGee*, you will find any record you can remember here. Memory Music, 133 E. Wall in Sherman, is the culmination of a lifetime of collecting for owner Roy Vickrey. His dad played the fiddle, guitar, banjo and harmonica, and his mom played the piano. So, he grew up surrounded by music. Roy's music collection includes almost 50,000 records—45s, 78s and LPs—and more than 1,000 matted and framed pieces of music memorabilia. Roy creates unique pieces of art by framing records with their sleeves or photos of the artists. These wonderful collectibles make treasured gifts. The store is open Wednesday-Saturday 9 am-6 pm. Contact Roy at 903-821-9038.

Ventura's

With a philosophy that "your surroundings should be a reflection of your personal style," Janet Ventura provides the perfect place to help you define just what that style might be. Ventura's, 1800-L N. Travis, is an extraordinary collection of beautiful things for the home and holidays. It is a "one stop" shopping experience, where you will find everything for any room in your home. Her brightly colored mix and match china and pottery lines make getting together with family and friends a delight. The designs are casual and functional, yet fun and easy. Janet says that the only hard part is deciding which style you love the most.

Collectors will delight in the large selection of some of the world's finest collectibles, including: Rochard Limoges, Swarovski, Byers' Choice Carolers, Chirstopher Radko, Lalique and many more. In the stationery department, you will find an extensive collection of greeting cards and in-house services for stationery and invitations. Brides receive a 20 percent discount on invitations when they register with Ventura's.

The store is overflowing with gleaming crystal, silver and pewter ware. A floral designer is on staff to create outstanding floral arrangements and gift baskets for special occasions. Your every gift giving need is met with professional attention to detail and unparalleled customer service. Ventura's is also a favorite place in Sherman to shop for holiday décor. The colorful and charming rooms come to life each season with the most enchanting gifts and accessories you can imagine. The store is open Monday-Saturday 10 am - 5:30 pm. Call 903-868-2656 or visit online at www.venturasgifts.com.

Restaurants

In 1996, the Menon family created what was soon to become a gourmet mainstay in a small, historic Texoma town. Housed in a renovated building of 1888, Blue Door Café is proud to be the only restaurant of its kind in the Texoma region, serving gourmet fusion dishes to people from around the world. Blue Door Café, 219 N. Travis in Sherman, has been recognized in *Texas Highways* magazine for its flavorful food and historic charm, and it continues to garner praise from visitors for its intimate decor and quality menu items. The Blue Door Café menu features something for everyone, from pork tenderloin and pecan-crusted chicken to a large selection of seafood and vegetarian dishes. Guests are asked to save room for the house specialty—Shanta Menon's famous bread pudding, topped with a sugary bourbon sauce. Bring your own wine to make your evening even more special. Blue Door Café is open Monday-Thursday 5-9 pm and Friday-Saturday 5-10 pm. For more information, call Blue Door at 903-893-5053.

Pull up a mismatched chair, grab a delicious cup of coffee, and find out the "downtown scoop!" Located in a 1920s building, The Muse, 225 S. Travis in Sherman, is an eclectic restaurant and coffee shop where you can find "something great, something different, something healthy, or something quite sinful." Owners Shannon and Lancel King, and John Lively offer pickup or free delivery, catering at the office or home, and a wonderful ambiance to enjoy breakfast, lunch or decadent desserts. The menu features warm breakfast dishes, great salads and sandwiches, and our favorite, Chocolate Disaster for dessert. Many customers even keep their own coffee cup at The Muse. The restaurant is open Monday-Friday 7 am-2 pm and by reservation for special occasions. For more information, call 903-891-3995.

Discover Waxahachie

It is called "The Crape Myrtle Capital of Texas," "The Gingerbread City," and "The Movie Capital of Texas." Waxahachie opens its historic arms to more than 500,000 visitors each year who enjoy the city's rich culture and history. The historical "Shawnee Trail" ran right through the center of downtown, which is now surrounded by a myriad of antique and gift shops, boutiques and wonderful restaurants. Mr. E. W. Rogers owned the land upon which the town of Waxahachie was laid out. In fact, he built his first home during the 1840s upon the present site of what is now the beautiful and historic Rogers Hotel. By the time Waxahachie was formally incorporated in 1871, the town was already thriving. However, it really began to prosper with the arrival of the railroad in 1879. During that period, most of the present downtown area was built, as well as many of the beautiful historical homes and hotels. Visitors to Waxahachie love the opportunity to "step back in time" and catch a glimpse of "vintage America" and its legend that is alive and well today. Town leaders invite guests to "Come for the History, Stay for the Charm," and charming it is!

Bloomin' Waxahachie!

You cannot imagine the incredible, vibrant Crape Myrtle blooms that seem to drape the city of Waxahachie—firecracker red, vibrant watermelon and cotton candy pink, and creamy white crape myrtles color the city throughout the spring and summer, giving it the well-deserved title "The Crape Myrtle Capital of Texas." Visitors come from across the country to view the blooming extravaganza, which culminates with the Crape Myrtle Festival during the Fourth of July weekend. The festival and Driving Trail consists of a fireworks display, concert, parade, food and lots of beautiful blooms.

Are You Going To Scarborough Faire?

Waxahachie offers the perfect opportunity to experience the majesty of the 16th century Renaissance days of King Henry VII. It is called Scarborough Faire Renaissance Festival, and it is the most fun you'll have in this century! You will experience the spectacle of jousting knights, swashbuckling swordfighters and the Royal Falconer. More than 200 quaint "village shoppes" sell treasures and trifles, and artisans demonstrate their talents. Kids (of all ages) enjoy jugglers, magicians and even "bawdy wenches" on eleven stages, and you will feast on more than 60 types of food. Grab a turkey leg and join the fun! The festival is open Saturdays and Sundays from the second Saturday in April through Memorial Day.

The Gingerbread City

Known for its magnificent, ornate woodwork found on many of the historic homes and the Ellis County Courthouse, Waxahachie celebrates this distinct attraction with, of course, a celebration! The Gingerbread Trail Historic Home Tour, held the first full weekend in June, is an annual home tour sponsored by the Ellis County Museum. Five intricately carved homes and the beautiful courthouse are featured on each tour. During this time, the downtown historic area comes alive with an arts and crafts fair.

Picture Perfect Waxahachie!

With its beautiful rolling hills, picturesque courthouse square, gingerbread homes and fields of breathtaking bluebonnets, Waxahachie has developed into the "picture perfect" location for more than 30 motion pictures or made-for-TV movies and specials. This includes three that were Academy Award winners. The first major motion picture to be shot in Texas was "Giant" during the 1960s, and since then Hollywood has fallen in love with the Lone Star State—especially the historical town of Waxahachie. It is considered one of the top spots in the nation for film and video production. You will, of course, recognize the award-winning movies "Tender Mercies" with Robert Duvall, "Places in the Heart" with Sally Field, and "Bonnie and Clyde" with Warren Beatty and Faye Dunaway. Other notable films shot here include "Of Mice and Men," "Cowboy," "Ellie," "The Trip to Bountiful," "The All-American Cowboy," "It Takes Two," "River Bend," "Born on the Fourth of July," and one of every Texan's favorites, "Pure Country" with George Strait. Indeed, the town has certainly earned its title as "The Movie Capital of Texas!"

"Come For The History, Stay For The Charm!"

Waxahachie eagerly awaits your visit. The people are proud of their city and the legend it has become in its own time. You'll find that they celebrate life every chance they get. You will love discovering, as we did, the delightful little shops and boutiques, and the charming cafés and restaurants. Most of all, you will enjoy meeting the friendly folks who have the honor of calling Waxahachie their home.

For more information about Waxahachie, contact the Waxahachie Chamber of Commerce at 972-937-2390, or visit www.waxahachiechamber.com or www.waxahachie.com online.

Waxahachie Fairs Festivals & Fun

April
Scarborough Faire Renaissance Festival

May
Scarborough Faire Renaissance Festival
Lions Mini Grand Prix Race

June
Gingerbread Trail Historic Home Tour and Arts & Crafts Sale
Gingerbread Golf Classic
Juneteenth Parade and Celebration
Cow Creek Country Classic Bike Ride

July
Crape Myrtle Festival & Driving Trail

September
Chautauqua Assemblies
Texas Country Reporter Festival

October
Cotton Fest
Screams Halloween Theme Park

November
Candlelight Christmas Home Tour

December
Bethlehem Revisited
Christmas & All The Trimmings Craft Sale
Christmas Parade
Candlelight Christmas Home Tour

Artists & Art Galleries

Birthday parties and club meetings love gathering around the big project table at Mosaic Madness, 300 W. Main in Waxahachie. Here they are introduced to the exciting art of Mosaics. Owners/artists Wanda Hendrix and Kelly Francis offer mosaic items, mirrors, stained glass and candles, as well as evening classes. The studio is open Monday - Thursday 10 am - 6 pm, Friday until 9 pm and Saturday until 5 pm. For more information, call 972-937-5797 or visit www.mosaicmad.com.

Children's

Like the name? You'll absolutely *love* the store! Chickadoodle, 507 N. Hwy 77, #804 in Waxahachie, is as fun and imaginative as its whimsical name. Tresa Bigham's husband and children named the store, while every other member of her family is involved in making it the "coolest" children's boutique in town. Kids of all ages love shopping Chickadoodle for the wonderful selection of the very latest trends in clothing and accessories, and new mommies love all of the soft, cuddly, baby items. Tresa carries Little Giraffe, a line of soft chenille blankets—the softest you will ever touch—and offers monogramming. We loved the personalized nap mats, hooded towels and chenille burp cloths—perfect for baby showers! The displays are always changing, and the entire store is bright and cheerful. Store hours are Monday - Saturday 10 am - 6 pm. Call 972-935-0770 to learn more.

THE PONY EXPRESS You'll think you've gotten on the wrong stagecoach and ended up way out West when you visit this wonderful clothing and accessory shop in downtown Waxahachie. The Pony Express, 213 W. Jefferson St., is a unique and wonderful store that can best be described as "a crossover between contemporary and western fashion." Owner Tish Creech loves to "mix things up" and create new looks that make everyone feel comfortable and beautiful.

The Pony Express began back in 1997 as the Clear Fork River Company—a family-owned business that traveled to small trade shows. As the company grew through the years, the mother, father and daughter team moved into the W. Jefferson building and opened The Pony Express. The daughter, Tish, now manages the store, and has developed it into a high-end retail shop featuring clothing, handmade jewelry and home décor. She carries only top quality, handmade products from New Mexico, Arizona, Montana, Texas and Mexico.

The sounds of country music fill the air and delicious candles burn, creating the perfect backdrop for some serious shopping! As you browse the store, you'll be amazed at the clever displays of beautiful items. Tish carries Double D. Ranchwear—a unique up-scale clothing line made in Yoakum, Texas and featured in the *Cowboys & Indians Magazine*, F.L. Malek, Ivy Jane, Telluride Clothing, British Khaki and Talusa Rose. You'll also find hand-made jewelry by Laura Scovio, who is featured in Saks Fifth Avenue.

The Pony Express is open Monday-Friday 10 am - 5:30 pm and Saturday 10 am-4:30 pm. For more information, visit www.theponyexpressonline.com online or call 972-937-5524.

Gifts & Home Décor

Sherrie and Dub Green have drawn from their many years of retail experience to create the "perfect shop." These Waxahachie natives have owned a family restaurant, an antique shop and after retiring from the lighting business, opened The Studio at 101 Tracy Ln. They started with rustic furniture and accessories and quickly added unique, trendy, fashion jewelry at the lowest possible prices. Sherrie and Dub travel to Mexico at least once a month, so the shop is always stocked with new items. And, because they are on the outskirts of town, they also have room for patio and iron pieces for the home and garden. Customers love the eclectic mix of merchandise from beautiful turquoise and coral to iron crosses and Texas décor, and they appreciate the great prices and discounts. The Studio is open Tuesday-Saturday 9 am-6 pm. Call 972-617-7740.

Jewelry

When you enter Maxwell Jewelry, it's like strolling back in time. Since 1946, three generations of Maxwells have owned and operated this unique shop where you can find fine jewelry, estate jewelry and jewelry repair. Owners John and Billie Maxwell make you feel like part of the family in the store's warm, friendly atmosphere. Located just off the square between two antique shops at 311 S. Rogers in Waxahachie, it's open 8 am - 5 pm Monday-Saturday. For more information, call 972-937-4381.

Maxwell Jewelry
WATCHES - DIAMONDS
OTHER FINE JEWELRY - JEWELRY REPAIRING

Restaurants

CAMPUZANO
mexican food

Enjoy sizzling fajitas, grilled shrimp in Diablo Sauce, delicious enchiladas and banana burritos at Campuzano Mexican Food, 2167 N. Hwy. 77 in Waxahachie. From the "World Famous Campuzano Nachos" to the wonderful Tacos al Carbon, everything is fresh and spicy! The favorite "Banana Burritos" are bananas wrapped in a thin pastry, lightly fried, rolled in sweet spices, topped with ice cream, whipped cream and warm chocolate sauce. Yum! Be sure to check out their other location at 213 W. Belt Line Rd. in Cedar Hill. Open daily, 11 am - 9 pm and Friday - Saturday until 10 pm. Call 972-938-0047.

Their goal—"to glorify the Good Lord who has truly blessed this shop," says owner Pam Carpenter. "The name of the shop, Just for You, relays the message that Christ died 'Just For You!'" You will feel the love of Christ shining through every staff member. Each one bubbles with the joy of the Lord. In fact, one of the stylists plays praise music at the piano whenever she has a spare moment! Just For You, 311 Ferris Ave., is located in a charming Victorian-style cottage near downtown Waxahachie. The house had partially burned down when Pam got her hands on it. Today, the warm, cozy, Victorian house exudes charm and comfort and feels more like a good friend's home than a spa. You'll feel right at home as soon as you walk through the doors. The front porch has been enclosed to house a wonderful little gift shop and boutique, where you'll find Susan Bristol clothing, Pine Cove Apparel, plus sizes by Hot Dames and Dermalogica skin care products. There are wonderful fashion accessories such as Inspirational Jewelry by Anita Goudeau Designs and body care items that make great gifts. Treat yourself or someone else!

Pam invites visitors to plan a special time to relax and enjoy all of the special treatments and indulgences. Her staff is professional and caring, and considers it a ministry to make everyone feel as relaxed and comfortable as possible. Whether you need nail or hair care, or a special skin-care treatment, you will be treated by the finest technicians who really care about your total health—spirit, soul and body. You'll enjoy being around such happy, dedicated people who love the Lord and love what they do! Just For You is open Tuesday-Saturday 8:30 am - 5:30 pm (or until you are ready to go!). For reservations or information, call 972-937-1910.

Specialty Shops

Pipers Gallery & Apothecary

Piper's Gallery & Apothecary is an unusual combination of original art and handmade items, as well as fresh herbs for healing, cooking and aromatherapy. Cheryl Kirkpatrick opened her store as a health and beauty source, but soon began incorporating wonderful hand-knitted hats, scarves and handbags—from traditional to Victorian. The store, 213 S. College in Waxahachie, is open Monday-Saturday 9:30 am-5:30 pm. Call 972-937-0010 or visit www.piperscrossing.com.

Index

Cross Reference

The Main Street Pub and Eatery – 157
T-Shirts N Texas Gifts and Souvenirs
  – 245
Venura's – 246
Wrap It Up – 126

Hotels/Motels
Hampton Inn Richardson – 231
Homewood Suites Hilton – 173
Hotel Crescent Court – 53, III, FC
The Corinthian Bed and Breakfast
  – 36, V

Interior Design
Ambrosia Vintage Vogue – 190
Antique & Design Center of North
  Texas – 142
Bacchus Floors – 210
Brenda's Antiques & Gifts – 241
Consign & Design – 125
French Dressing – 189
No Place Like Home – 124
Pierson's Fine Quilts – 77
Plaza Arts Center – 71
Sandaga Market African Imports – 35
Second Home Furniture – 169
Seconds & Surplus Building Materials
  – 47, 234
The Avenue – 226
The Wooden Swing Company – 38
Vine & Branches – 153

Jewelry
Anthurium Art Gallery – 185
Antiques East A Collection of Shops
  – 133
B Hive – 154
Barron's Fine Jewelry – 155, VI
Beads, Bags N Charms – 41
Beasley's Jewelry – 174
Bella Matiz – 154
Bella Rosa – 123
Brenda's Antiques & Gifts – 241
C.J. Riley & Co. – 188
Callidora – 43
Cardona & Campbell Jewelers – 115
Cotton Hearts – 187
Cynthia Elliott Boutique, Inc. – 188

Gainesville Factory Shops – 160
Glenda Kay's Gifts & Collectibles – 98
Irving Antique Mall – 114
It Spoke To Me – 183
J.R. & Co. – 42
Kinne's Jewelers – 156
Lancaster Town Square – 94
Liz Morgan Womens Fine Apparel – 40
Luanna's – 102
Mary Lou's Gifts & Collectibles – 75
Maxwell Jewelry – 256
McGillicuddy's Antiques – 226
Merle Norman Cosmetics & Boutique
  – 103
Nature's Finest Art – 205, VII
Paradise Cowboy – 102
Peek in the Attic – 51
Plaza Arts Center – 71
Southwest Corner Gallery – 97
Ten of Arts – 75
The Avenue – 226
The Little Red Hen – 187
The Ole Moon – 34
The Studio – 255
Two Divas – 42
Venura's – 246
Wrap It Up – 126
Zola's Everyday Vintage – 39

Museums
A Touch of Class Antique Mall – 240
Kinne's Jewelers – 156
Old City Park – 56
Plaza Arts Center – 71
The Women's Museum – 55

Pampered Pets
Lancaster Town Square – 94
Talulah Belle – 52

Quilts/Needlework/Stitchery
Carriage House Quilt Shoppe – 211
Knick Knacks Crafts & Antiques Mall
  – 96
McGillicuddy's Antiques – 226
Pierson's Fine Quilts – 77
Quilt Country – 175
The Antique Collection – 184

Dear Adventurer,

    If you are reading this book chances are you are an 'Adventurer.' An 'Adventurer' is a person with a sense of adventure and a curiosity for new and exciting places, people and experiences—both long and short distances. All of the Lady's Day Out books appeal to that sense of adventure and cater to the natural curiosity in all of us.

    A Lady's Day Out, Inc., would like to share this gift of the perfect combination between work and travel with our loyal following of readers.

    In an effort to expand our coverage area we are looking for adventurous travelers who would like to help us find the greatest places to include in our upcoming editions of A Lady's Day Out. This is a wonderful opportunity to travel and explore some of the best destination cities in the United States.

    If you would like more information, we would love to hear from you. You may call A Lady's Day Out, Inc. at 1-888-860-ALDO (2536) or e-mail us through www.aladysdayout.com online.

    Best wishes and keep on exploring, from all of us at A Lady's Day Out, Inc.

"A Lady's Day Out Giveaway" Entry Form

Have five of the businesses featured in this book sign your entry form and you are eligible to win one of the following: weekend get away at a bed and breakfast, dinner gift certificates, shopping spree gift certificates or $250 cash.

1. _____
   (NAME OF BUSINESS)   (SIGNATURE)

2. _____
   (NAME OF BUSINESS)   (SIGNATURE)

3. _____
   (NAME OF BUSINESS)   (SIGNATURE)

4. _____
   (NAME OF BUSINESS)   (SIGNATURE)

5. _____
   (NAME OF BUSINESS)   (SIGNATURE)

NAME: _____

ADDRESS: _____

CITY: _____ STATE: _____ ZIP: _____

PHONE#: _____ E-MAIL: _____

Where did you purchase book? _____

Other towns or businesses you feel should be incorporated in our next book.

_____

_____

No purchase necessary. Winners will be determined by random drawing from all complete entries received. Winners will be notified by phone and/or mail.

Mail To:
A Lady's Day Out, Inc.
8563 Boat Club Road
Fort Worth, Tx 76179

Fax To: 817-236-0033
Phone: 817-236-5250
Web-Site: www.aladysdayout.com